THE PRINCE

A Historical Critique

TWAYNE'S MASTERWORK STUDIES

Robert Lecker, General Editor

THE PRINCE
A Historical Critique

Victor Anthony Rudowski

TWAYNE PUBLISHERS • NEW YORK
Maxwell Macmillan Canada • Toronto
Maxwell Macmillan International • New York Oxford Singapore Sydney

Twayne's Masterwork Studies No. 82

The Prince: A Historical Critique
Victor Anthony Rudowski

Copyright © 1992 by Twayne Publishers
All rights reserved. No part of this book may be reproduced or
transmitted in any form or by any means, electronic or
mechanical, including photocopying, recording, or by any
information storage and retrieval system, without permission
in writing from the Publisher.

Twayne Publishers
Macmillan Publishing Company
866 Third Avenue
New York, New York 10022

Maxwell Macmillan Canada, Inc.
1200 Eglinton Avenue East
Suite 200
Don Mills, Ontario M3C 3N1

Macmillan Publishing Company is part of the Maxwell Communication
Group of Companies.

Library of Congress Cataloging-in-Publication Data

Rudowski, Victor Anthony, 1924–
 The prince : a historical critique / Victor Anthony Rudowski.
  p. cm. — (Twayne's masterwork studies ; no. 82)
 Includes bibliographical references and index.
 ISBN 0-8057-8079-3 : (alk. paper) : 20.95. — ISBN 0-8057-8555-8
(pbk. : alk. paper) : $9.95
 1. Machiavelli, Niccolò, 1469–1527. Principe. I. Title.
II. Series.
JC143.M3946R83 1992
320.1—dc20   91-34021
                                                           CIP

The paper used in this publication meets the minimum requirements
of American National Standard for Information Sciences—Permanence
of Paper for Printed Library Materials. ANSI Z3948-1984.∞™

10 9 8 7 6 5 4 3 2 1 (hc)
10 9 8 7 6 5 4 3 2 1 (pb)

Printed in the United States of America

Contents

A Note on the References and Acknowledgments	vii
Chronology: Niccolò Machiavelli's Life	ix

LITERARY AND HISTORICAL CONTEXT

1. Historical Context	1
2. The Importance of *The Prince*	9
3. Critical Reception	12

A READING

4. The Genesis of *The Prince*	21
5. A Side-Glance at the *Discourses*	26
6. Louis XII: The Hereditary Prince	34
7. Cesare Borgia: The New Prince	45
8. Five Roads to Power	59
9. Military Considerations	71
10. Human Nature and State Religion	85
11. The Pattern of History	96
12. Posthumous Notoriety of *The Prince*	108
Notes	117
Selected Bibliography	119
Index	125

A Note on the References and Acknowledgments

The quotation in chapter 7 from Machiavelli's letter dated 26 June 1502 is taken from Roberto Ridolfi's *The Life of Niccolò Machiavelli,* translated from the Italian by Cecil Grayson and published by the University of Chicago Press in 1963. All other quotations from Machiavelli's writings and correspondence are taken from *The Chief Works and Others,* translated and edited by Allan Gilbert and published by Duke University press in 1965. The map of north-central Italy in Machiavelli's time is reproduced from *"The Prince" by Niccolò Machiavelli: A Norton Critical Edition,* translated and edited by Robert M. Adams, with the permission of W. W. Norton & Company, Inc. Copyright © 1977 by W. W. Norton & Company, Inc.

Niccolò Machiavelli 1469–1527. Portrait by Santi di Tito.
Courtesy of Palazzo Vecchio, Florence.

Chronology: Niccolò Machiavelli's Life

1469	Machiavelli is born 3 May in Florence. Lorenzo de' Medici (Lorenzo the Magnificent) assumes leadership of Florence at the age of 20.
1476–86	Receives the customary humanistic education, interrupted for 22 months by a course in commercial mathematics.
1487–95	May have spent most of this time at Rome employed by a Florentine banker.
1492	Rodrigo Lanzol y Borja (Borgia), a Spanish cardinal, is elected pope and will reign as Alexander VI. Lorenzo the Magnificent dies.
1494	Returns to Florence. Medici family is expelled from Florence and Girolamo Savonarola, a zealous member of the Dominican order, gains control of the city. King Charles VIII of France invades Italy.
1497	Savonarola's unremitting attacks on the Church for moral turpitude lead Pope Alexander to excommunicate him 18 June.
1498	Elected head of the Second Chancery, as well as secretary to the Council of Ten for War. Savonarola and two confederates are executed 23 May. Charles VIII dies; Louis XII is crowned king of France on 27 May. Pope Alexander grants Louis XII an annulment decree, enabling him to marry Anne of Brittany, widow of

	Charles VIII. In return, Louis makes military support available to Cesare Borgia, an illegitimate son of Pope Alexander.
1499	Louis XII invades Italy 10 August to enforce his hereditary claims on the duchy of Milan and the Kingdom of Naples.
1500	Machiavelli's father dies in May. Leaves Florence in July on his first diplomatic mission to the court of Louis XII in France and remains there for the rest of the year.
1501	Marries Marietta di Lodovico Corsini in August. A loyal wife and devoted mother, she would bear him six children, five of whom survived. Cesare Borgia is named duke of Romagna by his father, Pope Alexander.
1502	Cesare Borgia seizes the duchy of Urbino in June, and Machiavelli spends a few days there as a diplomatic emissary of the Florentine republic. In October he accompanies Cesare on a military campaign in Romagna, during which Cesare suppresses a conspiracy by his military captains in a way that wins Machiavelli's admiration.
1503	In August Cesare Borgia and his father are simultaneously struck with malaria. Pope Alexander dies, but Cesare recovers. Pius III, Pope Alexander's successor, dies in October after a reign of less than one month. Machiavelli is dispatched to Rome as an official observer at the election of the new pope, Giuliano della Rovere (Julius II). Machiavelli remains in Rome through the end of December and has several meetings with Cesare Borgia to discuss the political future of north-central Italy.
1504	Cesare Borgia is arrested and banished to Spain by Pope Julius.
1506	From January to August, Machiavelli raises, organizes, and trains a civil militia to make Florence less dependent on mercenary troops. From August to November he serves as the Florentine representative at the traveling court of Pope Julius on his military campaign to reassert papal authority over Bologna and Perugia, whose papal vicars, Machiavelli observes, are no match for the warrior-pope.
1507	Cesare Borgia dies 12 March.
1509	Florentine troops, including selected units of the civil militia, enter Pisa on 8 June after the city formally agrees to end its protracted struggle for independence.
1511	Pope Julius forms the Holy League to fight French expansion.
1512	On 14 September the Medici family is restored to power in Florence, and the republic is abolished. Less than two months later, Machiavelli is dismissed from the Second Chancery and the Council of Ten for War.

Chronology: Niccolò Machiavelli's Life

1513	In the spring Louis XII is forced to withdraw his forces from Italy. Machiavelli is wrongly accused 23 February of being part of a conspiracy to reestablish the republic and is tortured. Lack of evidence compels the authorities to release him. He decides to retire to his ancestral villa at Sant' Andrea.
1513	Cardinal Giovanni de' Medici is elected pope on 11 March after the death of Julius II and will reign as Leo X. The task of governing Florence is turned over to his brother Giuliano.
1513	Writes *The Prince*. After a Pyrrhic victory at Ravenna and other reverses, Louis XII withdraws his troops from Italy.
1515	Louis XII dies, still intervening in Italian affairs up to the time of his death. He is succeeded by Francis I.
1516	After some revision, Machiavelli presents *The Prince* to the pope's nephew, Lorenzo de' Medici, who has replaced the temperamentally unsuited Giuliano as governor of Florence.
1514–19	Completes the *Discourses*, a work apparently begun in 1513, and begins writing *The Art of War* and the poetic epic, *The Golden Ass*.
1518	His comedy in five acts, *The Mandrake*, is published.
1519	Following the premature death of Lorenzo de' Medici, Pope Leo turns over the governance of Florence to a nephew of Lorenzo the Magnificent, Cardinal Giulio de' Medici. Giulio commissions Machiavelli to write *The Florentine History* and entrusts him with a few minor diplomatic missions.
1520	Writes *The Life of Castruccio Castracani*.
1521	*The Art of War* is published. Makes his first diplomatic mission Tuscany since his exile when he is commissioned to go in May to a conclave of Franciscan friars at Carpi.
1521	Pope Leo dies 1 December and is succeeded by Hadrian VI.
1523	Cardinal Giulio de' Medici, under the name Clement VII, succeeds Hadrian VI 19 November.
1525	In mid-January his comedy *Clizia* is publicly performed in Florence. Journeys to Rome in the spring to present *The Florentine History* to Pope Clement. Urges the pontiff to form civil militias for the defense of Florence and Romagna.
1526	In April Pope Clement approves Machiavelli's idea of creating a commission, the Curators of the Walls, to oversee the reconstruction and fortification of Florence's walls; in May, he is elected secretary and quartermaster of the commission.
1527	Pope Clement's diplomatic mistakes lead to the sack of Rome in

May by mercenaries employed by the German emperor Charles V. The Florentines take advantage by expelling the Medici and reestablishing the republic. Machiavelli hopes to be reinstated to his former posts, but the new regime rejects him because of his previous association with the Medici. Machiavelli dies 21 June in Florence at age 56. On the next day his remains were interred in the private family chapel in the Gothic church of Santa Croce. There, a monument in his honor now bears the inscription: "No eulogy would do honor to so great a name" (*Tanto nomini nullum par elogium*).

LITERARY AND HISTORICAL CONTEXT

1

Historical Context

The year that marks the birth of Niccolò Machiavelli holds a special significance in the historical annals of Florence since it was also in 1469 that Lorenzo, the eldest son of Piero di Cosimo de' Medici, succeeded to the political leadership of this Tuscan city; he had become the ranking member of the Medici family after his father's untimely demise. It should be emphasized that the family's traditional preeminence in affairs of state, which dated back to 1434, did not rest on any hereditary form of aristocratic entitlement, since the mercantile establishment that controlled the city at that time took pains to maintain a constitutional system of government that was outwardly republican in structure. The source of Medicean power lay in the vast network of banks that the family operated throughout Italy and Europe, as well as in the extensive agricultural and mining enterprises that were under its control within the province of Tuscany. Even though Lorenzo was merely 20 years of age when he took over the stewardship of Florence upon the death of his father and was little more than 43 when he himself died, his record as a statesman is unsurpassed in the chronicles of the Italian Renaissance. He was, moreover, a discerning patron of the arts and letters as well as a distinguished poet and humanist scholar in his own right. In acknowledgment of his diverse merits, historians now commonly refer to him as Lorenzo the Magnificent.

The Prince

Throughout much of his life Lorenzo found it necessary to engage in diplomatic activities whose objective was to preserve the political independence of his native city. The Italian peninsula had lost its political unity in the aftermath of the fall of the Roman Empire, and its reunification was not fully achieved until the mid-nineteenth century. In Lorenzo's day there existed five states whose territorial and military resources enabled them to affect the political destiny of the entire peninsula. The northern sector of Italy was dominated by Milan, Venice, and Florence. Of these three city-states, Milan was a duchy under the control of military despots of the Sforza family. Venice and Florence, for their part, were nominally republics but mercantile oligarchies in actuality. In central Italy lay a vast domain called the States of the Church that extended from the Tyrrhenian Sea in the west to the Adriatic Sea in the east, all of which was theoretically subject to the temporal authority of the pope. Even more extensive was the Kingdom of Naples, which lay immediately to the south of the papal states. This vast realm, officially known as the Kingdom of the Two Sicilies because it included the island of Sicily, had long been ruled by a dynasty affiliated with the Spanish royal house of Aragon. While each of these five Italian states sought to extend its own sphere of influence, they all had a vested interest in preserving the precarious balance of power that prevailed throughout the peninsula, and each could be counted on to oppose any overly ambitious territorial expansion on the part of any of the others.

Relations between these rival states were further complicated by the persistent threat of military intervention from powers outside of Italy. Toward the end of the fifteenth century, France posed the most imminent threat to the area since the French monarchy held a valid hereditary claim to sovereignty over the Kingdom of Naples. Ironically, when King Charles VIII of France decided to enter Italy for the sake of reclaiming his Neapolitan inheritance, he did so at the behest of Lodovico Sforza of Milan. Lodovico, known as *il moro* (the Moor) because one of his Christian names was Mauro and he had a very dark complexion, was the uncle of Gian Galeazzo Sforza, the duke of Milan, for whom he had been acting as regent since 1476 when his seven-year-old nephew inherited the ducal title. Even after Gian Galeazzo had come of age, Lodovico still re-

Historical Context

fused to relinquish power to his nephew. Isabella, the ambitious wife of Gian Galeazzo, was determined to oust the usurper. To achieve this end, she solicited support from her grandfather, King Ferrante of Naples, and her father, Duke Alfonso of Calabria. Lodovico attempted to forestall Isabella's intrigues against him by inviting the French ruler to unseat the Aragonese dynasty in Naples and add the southern kingdom to the domain of France. King Charles, quick to respond to Lodovico's prompting, moved his forces into Italy in September 1494 and succeeded in occupying Naples in February 1495.

Alarmed by the easy success of Charles VIII's armies, the Spanish king Ferdinand II of Aragon and the German emperor Maximilian I of the Holy Roman Empire formed a coalition with several Italian states aimed at forcing the French to abandon Naples. Oddly enough, Lodovico Sforza himself had belatedly come to realize the dangers posed by Charles VIII's presence in Italy. Because Gian Galeazzo had died from a mysterious illness shortly after the entry of French forces into Italy, Lodovico was no longer acting as regent for his nephew but had now become duke of Milan in his own right. In view of the altered circumstances, Lodovico eagerly joined the papal states and Venice in a newly formed anti-French coalition. Fearing his army would be cut off in Naples, Charles VIII ordered the greater part of his forces to beat a hasty retreat back to France. At Fornovo, on the Taro River in the vicinity of Parma, 34,000 Venetians and Mantuans sought to block the retreat of the main contingent of the king's forces. Even though the 8,000 French and Swiss troops under the command of Charles VIII in this encounter managed to inflict 3,500 Venetian and Mantuan casualties at the cost of only 100 on their own side, they had to abandon the baggage train during the confusion of battle and thus lost all the booty that was being transported back to France.

Of all the major peninsular powers, it was in Florence that Charles VIII's invasion of Italy had the most profound political impact. At that time the political leadership of the city was in the hands of Piero de' Medici, the eldest of Lorenzo's three sons. Unfortunately, Piero possessed little of the diplomatic talent for which his recently deceased father had been justly renowned throughout Italy. He responded to the crisis at first by entering into an alliance with Naples and the papal states that was formed to thwart Charles VIII's territorial claims in Italy. But, as soon as the forces of the French king entered the province of Tuscany and began to advance on Florence, Piero made a sudden reversal in policy. In a state of panic, he rode out to the French camp and placed himself at the mercy of King Charles. He agreed not only to surrender most of the major Tuscan fortresses to the invader but also to contribute the sum of 150,000 gold ducats toward defraying the cost of the French expedition against Naples. Upon returning to the city, Piero found that his abject capitulation to the invader was totally unacceptable to the members of the city council, as well as to most of the Florentine populace. Riots ensued, and Piero along with his two brothers fled Florence. The city council, known as the *Signoria,* thereupon decreed that the Medici family be banished from Florence forever and even offered a reward of 4,000 florins for Piero's head. While the *Signoria* subsequently succeeded in reducing the financial indemnity imposed by Charles VIII to 120,000 ducats and in obtaining some tentative assurances that the surrendered fortresses would ultimately be returned, it found itself obliged to accept most of the other terms entered into by Piero.

In spite of all the burdens imposed on Florence by Charles VIII, not all of its citizenry reacted adversely to the French incursion. Most supportive of King Charles were the followers of Girolamo Savonarola, an austere Dominican friar who originally came to Florence from his native city of Ferrara. The French monarch, in Savonarola's view, was no less than an instrument of the divine will by means of which Florence and the rest of Italy were destined to be redeemed from iniquity and restored to Christian virtue. In the period immediately following the expulsion of the Medici, Savonarola actually made considerable headway in mitigating the dissolute moral climate that pervaded the city of Florence. Most notably, he put a stop to the licentious activities that prevailed during the annual pre-Lenten carnival festivities, which he transformed into religious pageants in which the Florentines consigned "vanities" to sacrificial bonfires for destruction. Savonarola had considerably less success, however, with his mission to purify the corrupted Roman Catholic Church. His adversary in this struggle was none other than the Spaniard Rodrigo

Historical Context

Lanzol y Borja (Borgia), whose reign under the name Alexander VI is generally conceded to represent the moral nadir of the papacy during the Italian Renaissance. Savonarola's persistent challenges to papal authority finally led to his excommunication in 1497, an event which emboldened the friar's political adversaries to take direct action to destroy him. Savonarola and his two closest confederates in the Dominican order were placed under arrest and subsequently confessed to the charge of heresy after being severely tortured. On 23 May 1498 Savonarola and his two companions were escorted to the square in front of the Palazzo della Signoria (now called Palazzo Vecchio) and hanged atop a pile of brush and logs that was thereupon set ablaze by the hangman. Several hours later, the charred remains of the three men were gathered up and tossed into the Arno River. Machiavelli witnessed Savonarola's rise and fall at first hand and viewed the episode as an object lesson in the danger of being "an unarmed prophet."

Within a few months after Savonarola's death, the peace of Italy was once again disrupted by a military invasion on the part of the kingdom of France. Louis XII, who had succeeded to the French throne after the death of his cousin Charles VIII, decided to reassert his own hereditary claims to the duchy of Milan and swiftly deposed Lodovico Sforza as its ruler during the summer of 1499. King Louis was also resolved to incorporate the duchy of Brittany into his hereditary domain. To achieve this end, he needed to divorce his current wife and marry the widow of his predecessor, Anne of Britanny. Obviously, these unorthodox marital maneuvers required sanction by the papacy. The reigning pontiff, Alexander VI, duly granted approval in exchange for a pledge of French military assistance on behalf of Cesare Borgia, one of several illegitimate children he had fathered over the years by various mistresses.

Cesare Borgia, with the full backing of Pope Alexander, was intent on creating a state of his own with its nucleus in Romagna, a region along the Adriatic Sea in north-central Italy that includes such cities as Bologna, Faenza, Forlì, Imola, Ravenna, and Rimini. Although Romagna was at that time a constituent part of the States of the Church, its cities had long been under the control of petty tyrants who paid little heed to the authority of the pope. Named duke of Romagna by his father in 1501,

Cesare Borgia embarked on a campaign of conquest in which he subjugated the cities of the region one by one. In his zeal to expand his realm, he also made incursions into Tuscan territory, and it eventually proved necessary for Louis XII to intercede on behalf of his Florentine allies. The French king enjoined Cesare Borgia to withdraw his troops from Tuscany, and the problem of Florence's security was thereby resolved for the moment.

In view of the precarious political circumstances prevailing throughout the peninsula, however, the Florentines concluded that it was essential for them to enhance the authority of their chief executive official. The tenure of the *gonfaloniere della guistizia* (gonfalonier or standard-bearer of justice) had been restricted to a brief term in office by constitutional statute. In 1502, in imitation of the prerogative vested in the office of the Venetian doge, it was decided that the gonfalonier should have this appointment for life. The man whom the *Signoria* selected for the honor of serving as gonfalonier for life was Piero di Tommaso Soderini, a man whose fervor was instrumental in bringing about the downfall of the Medici and the restoration of the erstwhile Florentine republic.

As gonfalonier for life, Soderini was fortunate to be able to draw on the political expertise of Niccolò Machiavelli. Machiavelli had served as head of the Second Chancery and as secretary to the Council of Ten for War ever since the summer of 1498, when Savonarola and his two confederates had been executed. It still remains unclear why an inexperienced young man of 29 from an old but impoverished family should have been elevated to these key offices. Despite his youth and inexperience, however, Machiavelli was routinely commissioned to undertake sensitive diplomatic missions to other Italian states as well as to the courts of Louis XII in France and Maximilian I in Germany. Diplomatic activities such as these played a vital role in Machiavelli's development as an uncompromising exponent of political pragmatism.

Most instructive of all in Machiavelli's development as a political theorist were his extensive contacts with Cesare Borgia in Romagna. It was there that the Florentine secretary had the opportunity to observe firsthand the savage courage of this archetypal Renaissance prince. Cesare Borgia's meteoric political career was cut short suddenly, how-

Historical Context

ever, when both he and his father were simultaneously stricken by malarial fever, a malady endemic in Rome at that time. The elder Borgia succumbed to the illness within five days, but his son eventually recovered after hovering on the point of death for several weeks. The new pope, Pius III, died less than a month after his elevation to the Chair of Peter in 1503 and was succeeded by an inveterate enemy of the entire Borgia clan named Cardinal Giuliano della Rovere. Giuliano, who reigned under the name of Julius II, lost little time in removing the overly ambitious duke of Romagna from the Italian body politic. Within six months Cesare Borgia was arrested and banished to Spain, where he was killed a few years later in a minor military engagement while employed as a mercenary by the king of Navarre.

Pope Julius II, after having reclaimed the territory of Romagna on behalf of the papacy, proceeded to form a political coalition known as the Holy League, the aim of which was to drive Louis XII from the soil of Italy. This enterprise likewise proved successful, and the duchy of Milan was restored to the Sforza family in 1512. While Machiavelli strongly favored Florence becoming a member of the Holy League, Soderini refused to betray the trust of Louis XII and insisted on a policy of neutrality in the entire conflict. To punish the Florentine republic for its failure to support his anti-French crusade, Pope Julius deployed forces from the Holy League against the city and compelled its citizenry to accept the return of the Medici. Cardinal Giovanni de' Medici, the second eldest son of Lorenzo the Magnificent and the future Pope Leo X, entered Florence amid much ceremonial pomp on 14 September 1512 and promptly assumed full control of its government. Partisans of the Medici had already forced Soderini into exile at Siena, and Machiavelli himself was dismissed from office less than two months later. On 23 February 1513, moreover, Machiavelli was wrongly accused of being part of a conspiracy to reestablish the republic and put to torture on the rack. Even though lack of evidence compelled the authorities to release him after 22 days, he still feared rearrest and decided to retire to his ancestral villa at Sant' Andrea—a little village located seven miles from Florence and two from San Casciano—with his wife and children. Despite having to endure relative poverty while at Sant'

Andrea, Machiavelli managed to keep his intellectual faculties fully exercised by taking up the study of those Latin authors for whom he had developed an abiding affection during his adolescence. Fortunately for posterity, his premature retirement from public life at 43 furnished him the opportunity to write political, historical, and literary works of his own. Although Machiavelli regarded his exile from Florence as a great personal tragedy, it is difficult to envision any other circumstances under which he could have produced such major political treatises as *The Prince (Il principe)* and *Discourses on the First Ten Books of Titus Livius (Discorsi sopra la prima deca di Tito Livio)*.

2

The Importance of *The Prince*

Books offering advice to rulers constituted a well-established literary genre throughout the Medieval and Renaissance epochs. One of its most representative examples is the instructional manual that Desiderius Erasmus of Rotterdam published in 1516, *The Education of a Christian Prince (Instituo Principis Christiani),* a work dedicated to the Holy Roman emperor Charles V at the time of his elevation to the throne of Spain. As a youth, Machiavelli himself had received thorough training in the composition of formal letters purporting to advise individuals—sons, fathers, servants, masters, and princes—of the duties incumbent on them owing to their station in life. It was by means of this pedagogical exercise that humanistic educators united the study of classical rhetoric with a knowledge of practical affairs. A typical letter addressed to a prince would exhort him to defend the Christian faith, uphold the laws, keep his word, and practice charity—in short, to conduct himself in such a manner that his subjects would love him. Machiavelli delighted his contemporaries by inverting such moralistic platitudes through his insistence that it is far better for rulers to be feared than to be loved. Neither in *The Prince* nor elsewhere in his writings does he actually deny the validity of traditional moral values; he simply asserts that they are irrelevant to the conduct of affairs of state. From the vantage point of those who wield power, or hope to attain it, a treatise like *The Prince* is infinitely more helpful than one like *The Education of a Christian Prince*. Even though Erasmus's treatise had been personally dedicated to him, there is no evidence that Charles V ever paid any heed to it. On the other hand, Charles is known to have been a lifelong student of the Florentine's doctrines. According to contemporary reports, he kept three books beside his bed: the Bible, Baldassare Castiglione's *The Book of the Courtier (Il libro del cortegiano)* (1528), and Machiavelli's *The Prince*.

Machiavelli's singular achievement in writing *The Prince* lies in his having thereby initiated a pragmatic mode of political discourse that is entirely independent of ethical considerations derived from traditional sources of moral authority as embodied in classical philosophy and Christian theology. By the end of the sixteenth century, Machiavelli's approach to politics had crystallized into the doctrine of *raison d'etat*. (The phrase "reason of state" was apparently coined by Giovanni Botero and first appeared in print in its Italian form, *ragione di stato,* in a political treatise that he published in 1589.) According to this doctrine, it is permissible for a ruler to act in a manner contrary to the moral codes that govern relations between ordinary persons whenever the interests of the state are at stake. From this premise it can be argued that the perennial moral conflict between ends and means loses its validity in the sphere of politics. By the same token, some of Machiavelli's critics have charged that he is a teacher of evil and that *The Prince* is little more than "a handbook for dictators."

It is, of course, true that many tyrants have acknowledged their indebtedness to this treatise and have spoken highly of its contents. Among twentieth-century dictators it was Benito Mussolini who most openly proclaimed himself a staunch adherent of Machiavelli's views on the art of statecraft. On one occasion he wrote: "I believe Machiavelli's *Prince* to be the statesman's supreme guide. His doctrine is alive today because in the course of four hundred years no deep changes have occurred in the minds of men or in the actions of nations."[1] The extent to which Mussolini's actions, or those of any other ruler, were affected by his sympathetic reading of *The Prince* is, of course, impossible to determine. Machiavelli, after all, never invented Machiavellianism. It may be argued

The Importance of The Prince

that he saw himself as merely describing how men who succeed in attaining power, and in holding on to it, actually behave. Nonetheless, his doctrines do sanction the commission of ethically repugnant acts on behalf of a higher political goal and, as such, have contributed to the creation of a climate of opinion that enabled followers of tyrants like Joseph Stalin, Adolf Hitler, and Benito Mussolini to condone the immoral deeds of their leaders. Anyone who wishes to pass judgment on the morality of any of the ideas espoused in *The Prince* must likewise bear in mind that Machiavelli himself subscribed to a higher political goal that he believed was beyond considerations of good and evil: namely, the establishment of a unified Italian state that would be strong enough to expel the French, Spanish, and German interlopers. Accordingly, his vision of a unified Italy was a source of inspiration to such men as Camillo di Cavour, Giuseppe Mazzini, and Giuseppe Garibaldi who led the movement for unification called the *Risorgimento* (resurrection) that began about 1750 and lasted until 1870 when an army of Italian patriots entered the city of Rome amid the plaudits of the citizens.

3

Critical Reception

Machiavelli's political writings have elicited an unusual number of disparate reactions over the course of time. The first important critique of his views came from the pen of a fellow Florentine named Francesco Guicciardini, who was more than 20 years his junior. Guicciardini, a preeminent Italian historian, first met Machiavelli in 1520, and the two men took an immediate liking to each other. Some of Guicciardini's observations on Machiavelli's historical theories are conveyed in their correspondence; his main assessment, however, is contained in a treatise written several years after his friend's death, *Considerations on the Discourses of Machiavelli (Considerazioni sui discorsi del Machiavelli)*.[2] Despite the fact that this treatise deals specifically with the *Discourses*, much of Guicciardini's commentary is equally applicable to *The Prince* since Machiavelli's theoretical presuppositions in these two works are identical. Guicciardini does not attempt to survey the *Discourses* as a whole, however; he discusses only 38 of its 142 chapters. Even though both men subscribe to a cyclical view of history and believe in the superior merits of the republican form of government, they are divided on many important issues. For one thing, Guicciardini is highly critical of his friend's faith in the past as a guide to the present and the future. He concedes that patterns may exist but insists that explicit analogies between past and present political situations have no utilitarian value whatsoever. Nor does he share Machiavelli's conviction that the political organization of the Roman republic should serve as a model for contemporary governmental bodies. Guicciardini finds only the military discipline of the Roman citizenry worthy of emulation. Moreover, Machiavelli's view of humankind as an innately corrupt species runs counter to Guicciardini's belief that human nature, though frail, is basically good.

The next noteworthy commentary on Machiavelli by a European of major intellectual stature is to be found in Sir Francis Bacon's *The Advancement of Learning*, a treatise first published in 1605. Midway through book 2, for example, he hails Machiavelli as a fellow empiricist and maintains "that we are much beholden to Machiavel and others, that write what men do and not what they ought to do."[3] Similarly, Bacon goes on to praise the manner in which Machiavelli employs the principles of induction: "The form of writing which of all others is fittest for this variable argument [of inductive reasoning] is that which Machiavel chose wisely and aptly for government; namely, *discourses upon histories or examples*. For knowledge drawn freshly and in our view out of particulars, knoweth the best way to particulars again."[4] Near the end of book 2, however, Bacon takes care to disassociate himself from Machiavelli on the importance of genuine virtue in a ruler. He paraphrases Machiavelli on this point: "As for evil arts, if a man would set down for himself that principle of Machiavel, *that a man seek not to attain virtue itself, but the appearance only thereof; because the credit of virtue is a help, but the use of it is cumber.*[5] Bacon, for his part, firmly believes that an individual ought not to sacrifice virtue to ambition since its loss not only subverts one's self-esteem here on earth but will also meet with divine censure in the hereafter.

Among the next generation of English writers to come under the influence of Machiavelli was James Harrington, a political scientist whose best-known work is the utopian tract *The Model of the Commonwealth of Oceana* (1659). Like Machiavelli, whom he describes as "the only Politian of the later Ages," Harrington prefers the republican form of government to all others because it is founded on the principle of civic virtue—that is, a widespread ability on the part of the citizenry to equate its own interests with those of the state. He does, however, take issue with his mentor on several key issues. Perhaps his most serious disagreement with Machiavelli pertains to the role of the gentry in a republic. Whereas Machiavelli perceives the gentry and the common people as natural enemies, Harrington believes that the interests of these two social classes could be reconciled if the amount of property held by the gentry were limited and fixed forever through legislative enactment. Accordingly, the republic would then be permanent and its citizenry free of corruption. He thus rejects the cyclical view of history espoused by Machiavelli, in which republican and monarchical systems of government inevitably alternate over the course of time. Nonetheless, he still played a key role in promoting a true appreciation of Machiavelli's doctrines by the English-speaking public during the seventeenth and eighteenth centuries. Harrington's influence in this regard has been thoroughly examined in Felix Raab's *The English Face of Machiavelli* (1965) and in J. G. A. Pocock's *The Machiavellian Moment* (1975). Whereas Raab focuses on Machiavelli's role in effecting a decline in the importance of religion in the development of modern political theory, Pocock turns his attention to the revival of republican thought in Puritan England and in Revolutionary America. Pocock uses the phrase "the Machiavellian moment" to denote the moment and manner in which Machiavellian thought first made its appearance in Renaissance Italy, as well as to denote the moment at which any republic must confront the problem of maintaining its moral and political stability amid a stream of irrational events.

It is generally acknowledged that the first comprehensive analysis of the Florentine secretary's life and work is to be found in Thomas Babington Macauley's essay "Machiavelli," a work which first appeared in the March 1827 issue of the *Edinburgh Review*. Here, Macauley begins by conceding the nefarious reputation of his subject in a trenchant passage that runs as follows:

> We doubt whether any name in literary history be so generally odious as that of the man whose character and writings we now propose to consider. The terms in which he is commonly described would seem to

Critical Reception

import that he was the Tempter, the Evil Principle, the discoverer of ambition and revenge, the original inventor of perjury, and that, before the publication of his fatal *Prince*, there had never been a hypocrite, a tyrant, or a traitor, a simulated virtue, or a convenient crime.... Out of his surname they have coined an epithet for a knave, out of his Christian name a synonym for the Devil.[6]

As a first step in rehabilitating Machiavelli's reputation, Macauley underscores the exemplary nature of his subject's personal life. He then draws attention to Machiavelli's unselfish career as a civil servant and lifelong advocacy of republican government and Italian independence. To those who are troubled by Machiavelli's condonation, even outright sanction, of treachery and murder within the sphere of statecraft, Macauley recommends that the Florentine secretary be viewed as a product of his times, when such acts were customary among those vying for political power. He also suggests that his countrymen's adverse reaction to Machiavelli's doctrines may be due in part to the innate temperamental and moral differences between northern and southern Europeans. As to the character of specific works, Macauley writes: "The *Prince* traces the progress of an ambitious man, the *Discourses* the progress of an ambitious people."[7] Both treatises, he further contends, make the common error of placing the good of the state over that of its citizenry, for Machiavelli fails to recognize with sufficient clarity the great principle that societies and laws exist only for the purpose of increasing the sum of private happiness. Even so, Macauley holds that the precepts which may be culled from Machiavelli's writings excel those of all other authors "because they can be more readily applied to the problems of real life."[8]

Jean-Jacques Rousseau, writing nearly seven decades before the publication of Macauley's essay on Machiavelli, offered a novel interpretation of *The Prince* in the course of an analysis of monarchical government in the treatise *On the Social Contract (Du contrat social)* (1762). In chapter 6 of book 3, Rousseau asserts: "While pretending to give lessons to kings, he gave great ones to the people. Machiavelli's *The Prince* is the book of republicans."[9] The same point is made by the renowned Marxist writer Antonio Gramsci, whose *Prison Notebooks*

The Prince

(Quaderni del carcere) (1949–56) contains an extensive essay, "Notes on Machiavelli, on Politics, and on the Modern State" (*"Note sul Machiavelli, sulla politica, e sullo stato moderno"*). Gramsci contends that *The Prince* is really addressed to "those who do not know"—that is, the democratic citizenry of his own time—in the hope of educating it about the political techniques employed by the ruling class so that it might become the ruling class of the future.[10] Machiavelli's greatness, he further maintains, consists in his divesting politics of spurious ethical considerations. Gramsci's essay, originally written during the 1930s, was posthumously published in 1949. An English translation, however, did not appear in print until 1971.

A strikingly similar assessment of Machiavelli may be found in James Burnham's *The Machiavellians: Defenders of Freedom* (1943). As Burnham defines its purpose, this book constitutes a defense of political truth as represented by the views of Machiavelli and an attack on wishful thinking as typified by Dante—a distinction based on the former's ability to divorce politics from ethics and the latter's inability to do so. Burnham also credits Machiavelli with a full understanding that politics is primarily the study of the struggles for power among men. Consequently, if knowledge of Machiavelli's political precepts were widely disseminated among the citizenry of any state, the success of tyranny and all other forms of oppressive political rule would be greatly diminished. Burnham goes on to argue that Machiavelli's relevance for our own time is in reminding us to keep strict watch over government officials and to make them subservient to the rule of law. Accordingly, it is precisely because he exposes the modus operandi of tyrants that Machiavelli has been defamed by the political establishment over the course of centuries. After his sympathetic, albeit by no means uncritical, exposition of Machiavelli's doctrines, Burnham gives an account of a group of political theorists whom he calls the modern Machiavellians: Gaetano Mosca, Georges Sorel, Robert Michels, and Vilfredo Pareto.

Another provocative interpretation of *The Prince* is Conor Cruise O'Brien's in *A Suspecting Glance* (1972). In the opening chapter he discusses "the ferocious wisdom of Machiavelli."[11] After conceding the Florentine secretary's deeply held commitment to republican virtues and

Critical Reception

genuine patriotism, O'Brien points out that there are a number of disquieting elements in his political philosophy that cannot easily be dismissed. There is, for example, Machiavelli's pronounced proclivity for violent and cruel solutions as reflected in his unabashed admiration for the bloody deeds of Cesare Borgia and the alleged inhuman cruelty of Hannibal. O'Brien also raises the question of whether Machiavelli was an Italian patriot who merely wished to see the "barbarians" expelled from his homeland or an inveterate imperialist who wanted his compatriots to subjugate alien peoples beyond the borders of Italy. In support of the latter view, O'Brien cites the sentiments Machiavelli expresses in "Tercets on Ambition" (*Dell'Ambizione*)—a long poem, composed in 1516, whose content has been grossly neglected in previous commentaries on *The Prince*. In subsequent chapters O'Brien discusses Friedrich Nietzsche's admiration for Machiavelli and Edmund Burke's opposition to the moral cynicism propounded in *The Prince*. The prime purpose of O'Brien's work is to encourage readers to cast "a suspecting glance" at the facile idealism of their own social and political beliefs by measuring them against the brutally realistic assessment of human nature that is to be found in the writings of Machiavelli and Nietzsche. Because of Machiavelli's open revolt against the exaltation of the intellect and reason that prevailed among most of his contemporaries, a number of cultural historians prefer to view his writings as a manifestation of the Counter Renaissance—a movement that included such disparate individuals as Martin Luther, John Calvin, and Michel de Montaigne, all of whom lived during the heyday of the Renaissance. As the content of O'Brien's *A Suspecting Glance* amply demonstrates, Machiavelli continues to be a disturbing figure in the cultural pantheon of Western man.

A READING

4

The Genesis of The Prince

Machiavelli's state of mind during his early years in exile at his estate in the village of Sant' Andrea is amply documented in his correspondence with the Florentine public official and historian Francesco Vettori. Five years younger than Machiavelli, Vettori decided to link his fortunes with those of the Medici after the fall of the republic in 1512 and was rewarded by being appointed Florentine ambassador at Rome. It is in a letter to Vettori dated 10 December 1513 that Machiavelli describes his life in exile most fully. After giving a detailed account of such matters as the entrapment of thrushes by means of birdlime and the sale of firewood cut in his grove, he writes:

> Leaving the grove, I go to a spring, and thence to my aviary. I have a book in my pocket, either Dante or Petrarch, or one of the lesser poets, such as Tibullus, Ovid, and the like. I read of their tender passions and their loves, remember mine, enjoy myself a while in that sort of dreaming. Then I move along the road to the inn; I speak with those who pass, ask news of their villages, learn various things, and note the various tastes and different fancies of men. In the course of these things comes the hour for dinner, where with my family I eat such food as this poor farm of mine and my tiny property allow. Having eaten, I go back to the inn; there is the host, usually a butcher, a miller, two

furnace tenders. With these I sink into vulgarity for the whole day, playing at *cricca* and at trich-trach, and then these games bring on a thousand disputes and countless insults with offensive words, and usually we are fighting over a penny, and nevertheless we are heard shouting as far as San Casciano. So, mixed up with these lice, I keep my brain from growing mouldy, and satisfy the malice of this fate of mine, being glad to have her drive me along this road, to see if she will be ashamed of it.

On the coming of evening, I return to my house and enter my study; and at the door I take off the day's clothing, covered with mud and dust, and put on garments regal and courtly; and reclothed appropriately, I enter the ancient courts of ancient men, where, received by them with affection, I feed on that food which only is mine and which I was born for, where I am not ashamed to speak with them and to ask them the reason for their actions; and they in their kindness answer me; and for four hours of time I do not feel boredom, I forget every trouble, I do not dread poverty, I am not frightened by death; entirely I give myself over to them.

And because Dante says it does not produce knowledge when we hear but do not remember, I have noted everything in their conversation which has profited me, and have composed a little work *On Princedoms*, where I go as deeply as I can into considerations on this subject, debating what a princedom is, of what kinds they are, how they are gained, how they are kept, why they are lost. If ever you can find any of my fantasies pleasing, this one should not displease you; and by a prince, and especially by a new prince, it ought to be welcomed. Hence I am dedicating it to His Magnificence Giuliano. Filippo Cassavecchia has seen it; he can give you some account in part of the thing in itself and of the discussions I have had with him, though I am still enlarging and revising it. (2:928–29)

The treatise identified in the above letter as *On Princedoms (De principatibus)* was later renamed *The Prince (Il principe)* when Machiavelli decided that an Italian title would be preferable to a Latin one.

The man named Giuliano to whom Machiavelli intended to dedicate his treatise on principalities was the youngest son of Lorenzo the Magnificent. Lorenzo himself once assessed the characters of his three sons by asserting that the eldest was foolish, the next clever, and the youngest good. The eldest, Piero, joined the French army after his expul-

The Genesis of The Prince

sion from Florence and was drowned while crossing the Garigliano River in 1503. The second son, Giovanni, was destined from childhood for the Church and achieved the rank of cardinal in 1492 shortly before the death of his father. As head of the Medici family when it returned to Florence, he became the de facto ruler of the city. After the death of Pope Julius II in the early months of 1513, Giovanni was elevated to the papacy as Leo X and turned over the governance of Florence to his younger brother Giuliano. It soon became apparent that Giuliano was temperamentally unsuited to exercise political authority over the city of Florence. He refused, moreover, to have any part in a scheme to unseat the reigning duke of Urbino, Federico Maria della Rovere, even though Giuliano himself was to be installed as the duchy's new ruler. Giuliano, who had lived at the court of Urbino for several years during the period of his exile from Florence, simply could not bring himself to do injury to those who had been so hospitable toward him. His tenure in office was to last less than three years. In 1516 Pope Leo replaced him with Lorenzo de' Medici, the 20-year-old son of his brother Piero. Shortly thereafter, Giuliano married Filiberta of Savoy and was named duke of Nemours by his wife's nephew, Francis I of France. Perpetually in ill health, Giuliano died almost immediately. Today he is chiefly remembered because of the idealized image of him carved by Michelangelo on the tomb that was commissioned in his memory by Leo X, a monument located in the New Sacristy at the Church of San Lorenzo in Florence.

Although Machiavelli completed *The Prince* in 1513, he continued to revise it for several more years. Sometime between September 1515 and September 1516 he wrote a dedicatory letter for the treatise that bears the salutation, "Niccolò Machiavelli to the Magnificent Lorenzo de' Medici." Machiavelli spares no effort to inform Lorenzo of his eagerness to serve him and concludes with the request:

> Accept this little gift, then, I beg Your Magnificence, in the spirit in which I send it; for if you consider it and read it with attention, you will discern in it my surpassing desire that you come to that greatness which Fortune and all of your own abilities promise you. And if from the summit of your lofty station, Your Magnificence ever turns your

eyes to these low places, you will perceive how long I continue without desert to bear the burden of Fortune's great and steady malice. (1:11)

Even though Machiavelli had been an ardent supporter of the republic headed by Soderini, he considered himself to be a professional civil servant above all else and burned with the desire to be of service to his native city. His treatise on principalities, he hoped, would convince Lorenzo of his political sagacity and thereby secure employment for him under the aegis of the Medici.

It is not known whether Machiavelli ever obtained an audience with Lorenzo to make a formal presentation of his treatise on principalities. According to a fairly reliable anecdote, however, Machiavelli made his presentation at a time when Lorenzo was being offered a pair of hunting dogs, and the gift of the dogs was received with far more favor than was the manuscript of *The Prince*. In any event, Lorenzo made no response to Machiavelli's appeal, and the erstwhile Florentine secretary was thenceforth denied the privilege of playing any role in the governance of his native city. As for the younger Lorenzo, he went on to conquer Urbino at the behest of Leo X and became its duke by papal investiture on 8 October 1516. Pope Leo had hoped to use his nephew to make the house of Medici a predominate power in Italian politics and to expel all foreigners from Italy through its agency. To achieve this end, the duchies of Ferrara and Urbino, along with the cities of Parma, Modena, and Piacenza, were to be united under the rule of Lorenzo. These plans came to naught, however, when Lorenzo died prematurely in 1519 at the age of 27. Cardinal Giulio de' Medici, a nephew of Lorenzo the Magnificent, succeeded him as ruler of Florence, and under Giulio's administration Machiavelli's fortunes improved somewhat. He was entrusted with a few minor diplomatic missions on behalf of the Medici, and more importantly, it was Giulio who commissioned Machiavelli to write *The Florentine History (Istoire fiorentine)*. Begun in 1520, shortly after Machiavelli had completed *The Art of War (Libro della arte della guerra)*, it was not officially presented to his patron in final form until 1525.

Giulio de' Medici was himself elevated in 1523 to the Chair of Peter, under the name Clement VII, when the immediate successor to Pope Leo

The Genesis of The Prince

expired after a brief reign of 20 months. A series of diplomatic missteps by Pope Clement led to the horrendous sack of Rome in 1527 by mercenaries in the service of the German emperor Charles V. The citizens of Florence took full advantage of the occasion by expelling the Medici from their own city and reestablishing the republic. Machiavelli believed that his time had finally come; he expected to be reinstated in the posts that he had held under Soderini. The Florentines, however, took a dim view of Machiavelli's previous association with the Medici and declined to entrust him with any posts in the new regime. Bitterly disappointed, Machiavelli died in Florence in 1527, a scant few months after the city had regained its liberty.

Since Pope Clement and Emperor Charles were quick to reconcile their differences, the eclipse of the Medici turned out to be of short duration. The Medici family returned to Florence in 1530, but this time they did so as a hereditary nobility. The city's days as an independent republic were thus ended forever.

5

A Side-Glance at the Discourses

Machiavelli, in the opening sentence of chapter 2, announces that he intends to restrict the scope of *The Prince* to issues pertaining to the governance and preservation of principalities: "I shall omit discussing republics because elsewhere I have discussed them at length" (1:11). The precise meaning of this reference to a treatise on republics has thus far proven difficult to establish with any degree of certainty. A few scholars have subscribed to the view that Machiavelli had already written a treatise on republics that was subsequently incorporated into the *Discourses on the First Ten Books of Titus Livius* as the opening 18 sections of book 1. The majority of scholars, however, believe Machiavelli was referring to the *Discourses* itself. Some of those who adhere to this position contend that Machiavelli had actually begun to write the *Discourses* earlier in 1513 and then set it aside to devote himself to the composition of *The Prince*. Others maintain that Machiavelli was merely speaking of his intention to write this opus sometime in the near future. Because it is nearly five times the length of *The Prince*, it is most probable that Machiavelli wrote the bulk of the *Discourses* between 1516 and 1519. Neither of these works, it must be noted, appeared in print before his death. The *Discourses* first appeared in print in 1531, and *The Prince* was published a year later in 1532. Copies of both

A Side-Glance at the Discourses

works, however, were widely circulated in manuscript form during Machiavelli's lifetime.

Livy, the name by which Titus Livius is commonly referred to in the English-speaking world, was born in the city now called Padua in 59 B.C. and died there in A.D. 17. Livy spent most of his life in Rome, where he worked for over 40 years composing a chronological history of Rome that commenced with its foundation by Romulus and Remus and culminated with its rise as the capital of an empire under the rule of Augustus Caesar. The work was arranged in groups of five and ten books called "pentads" and "decads," which were published in installments up until the time of Livy's death. Of the 142 books he composed, only 35 are still extant in whole or in part. Fortunately, abstracts for each book in the entire corpus were written sometime during the fourth century, and except for two pertaining to lost books, all of these have survived to the present day.

Despite the physical accessibility of most of this material during the Middle Ages, Livy's historical writings attracted relatively little attention from either churchmen or the educated laity. One of the few individuals to take a keen interest in Livy during that era was Dante Alighieri. Most notably, he frequently invokes Livy's authority throughout the treatise *On Monarchy (De monarchia)*. In canto 28 of *The Inferno*, moreover, Dante even speaks of the Roman historian's inerrancy (*Livio che non erra*). It was not until after Dante's death in 1321, however, that Livy's virtues became widely recognized owing to the efforts of humanists like Francesco Petrarca (Petrarch), Giovanni Boccaccio, Lorenzo Valla, and Angelo Polizano over the next 150 years. Because of his consummate literary merits, Livy exercised a profound influence on the prose style of many major writers who flourished during the Italian Renaissance. He was also one of the authors most favored by Michel de Montaigne, who frequently inserted passages from Livy into his essays.

Machiavelli, for his part, developed an abiding affection for the historical writings of Livy quite early in life. He was raised in a household consisting of his parents, two older sisters, and a younger brother. His mother, a young widow named Bartolomea Bennizzi née dei Nelli when she married his father, Bernardo, in 1458, was of a pious bent. Bernardo, a tax lawyer and petty landowner of modest means, was a man of pronounced scholarly proclivities with a genuine passion for Roman literature. Niccolò would take after his father.

Machiavelli's schooling in the principles of Latin grammar and rhetoric began just as he turned seven years of age. This course of study was interrupted about three and a half years later when his father enrolled him in a school that specialized in teaching a commercial form of mathematics known as *abbaco*. Twenty-two months later, having successfully completed the *abbaco* curriculum, Machiavelli once again resumed his schooling in the humanities, or what was then called *studia hūmānitātis*, which consisted of grammar, rhetoric, history, literature, and moral philosophy. This course of study involved the reading of classical Latin texts as well as Latin translations of Greek literature. A few schools of this type even studied some Greek texts in the original, but there is no evidence that Machiavelli ever received any formal training in the Greek language. Although the family was too poor to own many books, it did possess the extant writings of Livy. This survey of ancient Roman history must have been a favorite of both father and son since it was eventually sent to the bindery to be rebound when Niccolò Machiavelli was 17 years of age.

Little is known for certain about the next decade in Machiavelli's life. Some evidence has recently surfaced, however, indicating that he may have spent most of the years between 1487 and 1495 in Rome working for a prominent Florentine banker who operated a branch office there. If this was indeed the case, such proximity to the ruins of ancient Rome can only have intensified Machiavelli's long-standing interest in the writings of the man who was the foremost chronicler of its dramatic past.

It was, of course, more than admiration for the achievements of the Roman people that inspired Machiavelli's lifelong devotion to the historical writings of Livy. Of paramount importance to Machiavelli was that he and Livy shared a deeply rooted intellectual commitment to the republican form of government. Machiavelli originally intended to write on all of the extant books in Livy's survey of Roman history, but he never managed to get beyond the first decade (the tenth book of which concludes with the year 293 B.C.). Like Livy's writings, the *Discourses* are overtly didactic in tone. It is clear that the author's intent is to rouse his

A Side-Glance at the Discourses

compatriots to the kind of civic virtue that had once prevailed when the ancient Roman republic was establishing its dominion over the entire Italian peninsula. To achieve this end Machiavelli deems it necessary to invent an entirely new approach to historical writing. In essence, this new method consists of drawing parallels between ancient and modern history in the hope that the readers might learn lessons from the past and thus be better prepared to find solutions to the political and military problems confronting them in their own day. After all, he argues, the examples of the ancients had proven enormously beneficial in the realms of art, literature, medicine, and jurisprudence, so why not in the sphere of civil and military affairs? Convinced of the pioneering nature of his approach, Machiavelli announced that he was fully resolved "to enter upon a path not yet trodden by anyone" (1:190).

Despite Machiavelli's claim to originality, it has been suggested that he may have been inspired by the example set by Plutarch in his celebrated collection of biographies, *Parallel Lives*. This popular Greek author—of whom Ralph Waldo Emerson, in his lecture "Uses of Great Men," remarks that "we cannot read Plutarch without a tingling of the blood"—chronicled the lives of 50 famous historical figures from Greece and Rome. Four of these lives are dealt with individually, but the rest are arranged in pairs of contrasting Greeks and Romans. Thus, Theseus is paired with Romulus, Demosthenes with Cicero, and Alexander with Julius Caesar. Consequently, Machiavelli found in Plutarch a strong precedent for drawing parallels between different historical epochs. Moreover, it was while serving as a diplomatic emissary to Cesare Borgia during the fall of 1502 that Machiavelli is reported to have sent a message back to Florence requesting that a copy of Plutarch be sent to him. Hence, the idea of writing the *Discourses* may have originated at that time.

Upon completing the *Discourses*, Machiavelli decided to dedicate the work to a pair of private citizens named Zanobi Buondelmonte and Cosimo Rucellai out of gratitude toward them for unspecified benefits that they had bestowed on him in recent years. His bitterness toward Duke Lorenzo of Urbino for having failed to recognize the merits of *The Prince* is manifest throughout the dedication to the *Discourses*.

Even though not directly mentioned by name, Lorenzo is clearly on Machiavelli's mind when he spells out his reason for dedicating the *Discourses* to these friends of his rather than to a ruler:

> I believe I have got away from the common custom of those who write, who always address their works to some prince and, blinded by ambition and avarice, praise him for all the worthy traits, when they ought to blame him for every quality that can be censured. So in order not to run into this error, I have chosen not those who are princes, but those who because of their countless good qualities deserve to be; not those able to load me with offices, honors, and riches, but those who, though unable, would like to do so.

He concludes by addressing his friends directly: "Enjoy, then, that good or that ill that you yourselves have asked; and if you continue in the error of being pleased by these opinions of mine, I shall not fail to go through the rest of the *History*, as in the beginning I promised you. Farewell" (1:188–89).

Additional sardonic allusions to Lorenzo appear in the prologue to Machiavelli's comedy in five acts, *The Mandrake (La mandragola)*: "And if this material—since really it is slight—does not befit a man who likes to seem wise and dignified, make this excuse for him, that he is striving with these trifling thoughts to make his wretched life more pleasant, for otherwise he doesn't know where to turn his face, since he has been cut off from showing other powers with other deeds, there being no pay for his labors" (2:777–78). This tale of seduction, very much in the spirit of Giovanni Boccaccio's *Decameron* (1349–51), is generally acclaimed as the finest comedy to have been written in Italy during the Renaissance era, if not, indeed, in the entire history of the Italian theater. Although the precise date of composition is conjectural, it received its first publication in 1518. Thus, *The Mandrake* shares the distinction of being one of the two works by Machiavelli to have appeared in print during his lifetime. The other work—*The Art of War*—was subsequently published in 1521.

The staunch republicanism manifested in Machiavelli's *Discourses* may be best understood in the context of Florentine humanism. It was in

A Side-Glance at the Discourses

the writings of Leonardo Bruni, who served as chancellor of Florence from 1427 to 1444, that the arguments for the advantages of republican over monarchical government are set forth most unreservedly. Moreover, in an oration composed in Latin around 1401, *Panegyric to the City of Florence (Laudatio Florentinae urbis)*, Bruni challenges the widely held belief that the city of Florence had originally been founded by Roman legionnaires during one of Julius Caesar's military campaigns in north-central Italy. Partisans of ancient republicanism among the Florentine humanists considered the connection between Caesar and their city's origins to be totally inappropriate. After all, even though Caesar never formally invested himself with the royal crown, he did assume all the prerogatives of a monarch in point of fact and thus could be viewed as the principal agent of the Roman republic's final collapse. Bruni, accordingly, felt impelled to argue that the nation of Florentines arose at an earlier date, when the Roman people still enjoyed full civic freedom, and that its preeminent love of freedom and hatred of tyranny could be traced back to the noble republican traditions of ancient Rome.

Among his diverse intellectual distinctions, Bruni was also one of the foremost Greek scholars of his age; he translated many major works from the golden age of Greece into Latin. It was he, for example, who translated several of Plato's dialogues that were previously inaccessible to Europeans who lacked a reading knowledge of the Greek language. Of equal importance are Bruni's superior Latin renditions of Aristotle's *Nichomachean Ethics* and *Politics*. In the *Ethics* Aristotle defines happiness as the active exercise of the faculties of the soul in conformity with excellence or virtue; in the *Politics* he classifies man as a political animal by nature. For Bruni, as for Machiavelli, a full exercise of the human faculties had to include both *studia hūmānitātis* on the internal level and political activity on the external. Republics clearly offer far more opportunities to participate in politics than do principalities. The importance Machiavelli places on service to the state is most forcefully stated in his "Discourse on Remodeling the Government of Florence" (*Discorso per rassettare le cose di Firenze*), a work written about 1520 at the request of Pope Leo X:

> I believe the greatest honor possible for men to have is that willingly given them by their native cities; I believe the greatest good to be done and the most pleasing to God is that which one does to one's native city.... And so much has this glory been esteemed by men seeking for nothing other than glory that when unable to form a republic in reality, they have done it in writing, as Aristotle, Plato, and many others, who have wished to show the world that if they have not founded a free government, as did Solon and Lycurgus, they have failed not through their ignorance but through their impotence for putting it into practice. (1:113–14)

It is easy to understand why Machiavelli found it so traumatic to be removed from his post as a civil servant to the Florentine republic when the Medici returned to power in 1512.

One of the most important ways in which Machiavelli's political philosophy differs from the theories espoused by either Bruni or Aristotle lies in his belief that the strife of a continuing struggle between social classes may actually strengthen a state and promote the cause of liberty. In chapter 4 of book 1 in the *Discourses,* for example, he categorically rejects the view that Rome was a disorderly republic filled with confusion because of the perpetual strife between the plebians and the patricians: "I say that those who condemn the dissensions between the nobility and the people seem to me to be finding fault with what as a first cause kept Rome free, and to be considering the quarrels and the noise that resulted from those dissensions rather than the good effects they brought about; they are not considering that in every republic there are two opposed factions, that of the people and that of the rich, and that all the laws made in favor of liberty result from their discord" (1:202–3).

Machiavelli's commitment to civic liberty is by no means absolute, however. He freely concedes that the legal procedures normally used by a republic are far too cumbersome to be used in dire national emergencies, especially military threats from outside. In such circumstances, the full authority of the state needs to be vested in a solitary individual who is able to exercise kingly prerogatives with no interference from other citizens or officials—in short, a dictator. The Roman republic itself permitted the appointment of just such a dictator in times of trouble on the

A Side-Glance at the Discourses

condition that he was selected by the two chief magistrates (consuls), with the advice of the Senate, and that his term was limited to six months. Machiavelli has nothing but praise for the office of dictator and defends its utility in chapter 34 of book 1: "Certainly, among all Roman laws this is one deserving to be considered and counted among those causing the greatness of so powerful an empire, for without such a law the citizens have difficulty in escaping from strange and unexpected afflictions" (1:268). Since the post of dictator was intended to be strictly temporary, Machiavelli is utterly contemptuous of Julius Caesar's decision to make himself dictator for life and questions the judgment of those historians who feel otherwise. Not surprisingly, it is Brutus in his role as defender of the republic who is acclaimed by Machiavelli in the *Discourses*.

6

Louis XII: The Hereditary Prince

In the opening sentence of *The Prince,* Machiavelli asserts, "All the states, all the dominions that have had or now have authority over men have been or now are either republics or Princedoms" (1:11). Hence, the terms *prince, king,* and *monarch* are employed as synonyms throughout the treatise. Furthermore, Machiavelli makes no distinction between the office of a prince and that of a duke or a count. The only basic distinction he makes between a princedom and a republic is simply that power is exercised by one person in the former and by the many in the latter. It must be acknowledged, however, that in the *Discourses* he often appears to distinguish between a king and a prince. A king seems to be a monarch who administers his realm in accordance with long-established laws, whereas a prince is a ruler who either sets aside existing laws or creates new ones of his own. While Machiavelli never draws any overt distinction between these terms in *The Prince,* he does differentiate between rulers who are *hereditary* princes and those who are *new* princes.

The hereditary ruler whose career receives the most detailed analysis in *The Prince* is Louis XII, the immediate successor to Charles VIII as king of France. Both of these monarchs played a crucial role in the histor-

Louis XII: The Hereditary Prince

ical events that unfolded in the Italian peninsula during Machiavelli's lifetime. It was, in fact, Charles VIII's invasion of 1494 that opened the floodgates to armed intervention in Italian affairs by France, Spain, and Germany, climaxing with the 1527 sack of Rome. Quite likely, Charles VIII was the most unprepossessing monarch ever to be elevated to the French throne. He was a man of short stature with long scrawny legs, a large head, a short neck, a pair of globular eyes, and a great hooked nose that almost reached down to his coarse lips. His mental endowments were scarcely much better. He had just reached the age of 13 when his father, Louis XI, died in 1483, so a regency was established to rule on his behalf under his sister Anne of Beaujeu—a woman nine years older than he. She continued to serve as regent until 1491, however, even though her brother had reached his majority and was entitled to rule in his own right. Because of this prolonged adolescence, Charles had ample time to indulge his fantasies by reading chivalric romances and medieval French chronicles and contemplating such objects in the royal collection as the sword of Charlemagne and the armor of Jeanne d'Arc. Predictably, perhaps, he developed a consuming passion to acquire military glory for himself. He consequently decided to reassert a centuries-old claim to the Kingdom of Naples that his father had acquired when King Louis of Anjou died in 1480 without a male heir and all his holdings, both tangible and intangible, automatically reverted to the domain of the French monarchy. Since the Kingdom of Naples exercised sovereignty over the island of Sicily—a realm that carried with it a hereditary claim to the crown of Jerusalem—Charles reasoned that after securing possession of the Neapolitan throne he could also have himself declared king of Jerusalem and lead a crusade against the Turkish infidels who held the Holy Land in bondage. Hence, in the spring of 1494 Charles set out with a force of 18,000 cavalry and 22,000 infantry across the Alps to fulfill his destiny.

Although Charles expected to meet with serious resistance from some Italian states, his forces advanced with little or no opposition, and much of northern Italy soon fell under his control. He came by his triumphs so easily that Machiavelli was moved to assert in chapter 12 that the French monarch "was allowed to take Italy with chalk" (1:47). Machiavelli was referring to a remark made by Pope Alexander VI to the effect that the forces deployed by Charles often needed no weapons other than the chalk used by the quartermasters to mark the doors of the houses that were to serve as military billets for his troops. From Machiavelli's point of view, the main reason it was so difficult for the Italian principalities to stem the French advance was that they had entrusted their defense to mercenary soldiers rather than to a properly constituted civil militia. In offering this explanation, he also heaps scorn on Savonarola's contention that the tragic plight of Italy was attributable to its moral iniquity: "And he who used to say that the cause of it was our sins told the truth, but they were not at all such as he supposed they were, but these I have mentioned; and because they were princes' sins, the princes have suffered punishment for them" (1:48). There can be little doubt, moreover, that when Machiavelli wrote this passage, he had the fate of Piero de' Medici uppermost in his mind. But things eventually turned out badly for Charles despite his initial successes. When it appeared that his forces would be cut off in Naples, the French monarch retreated posthaste back to the safety of his homeland and considered himself fortunate to have escaped from Italy with his life. Altogether, Charles's sojourn in Italy lasted one and a half years.

In the years immediately preceding the French invasion of Italy, both Charles and his sister Anne were preoccupied with the political status of Brittany—an ancient province located in the northwestern region of present-day France. During the fifth and sixth centuries, this province received a large influx of Celts from Britain who were fleeing from the Saxon invaders of their homeland. Its language, Breton, bears a strong linguistic affinity with Welsh as well as with the extinct Cornish variant of Brythonic speech. By the end of the Middle Ages the ranking members of the aristocracy that governed the province had been thoroughly acculturated by their French-speaking neighbors. Nonetheless, they strongly resisted any and all attempts by France to deprive Brittany of its

Louis XII: The Hereditary Prince

independence. This struggle came to a head during the closing decades of the fifteenth century when it became clear that the duke of Brittany, Francis II, would be succeeded by his daughter, Anne, in the absence of a male heir. Hence, the question of selecting a suitable husband for Anne became a matter of critical importance. As a child she had been formally betrothed by proxy to Emperor Maximilian of Germany, who at the time of the engagement was still unmarried owing to the death of his first wife. The idea of a foreigner becoming ruler of Brittany, however, proved totally unacceptable to partisans of a strong, centralized French monarchy. After much political and military turmoil following the death of Francis II, Anne of Brittany was finally persuaded to marry King Charles himself, and the wedding between them took place in 1491.

The political association between Brittany and France that came about through this marriage was technically known as a personal union and hence did not necessarily entail an irrevocable loss of sovereignty on the part of the duchy. Specifically, the union between Brittany and France was to be automatically dissolved if Charles preceded the queen in death without leaving any children from the union to succeed him. To guard against this possibility, a clause was inserted into the marriage contract stipulating that in such an eventuality Anne would be obliged to marry his successor as king of France.

Charles and Anne did, in fact, have three sons, but all of them died in infancy. As for Charles himself, the hapless monarch died prematurely in 1498 at the age of 28 as the result of a concussion he suffered when he cracked his head on the lintel while passing under a low doorway. The closest heir to the French crown turned out to be Louis, the duke of Orléans. Unfortunately, Louis was already married to Jeanne of Valois, one of the sisters of the late king. She was a worthy and pious woman but plain in appearance. Louis had already ceased to live with her, and they had no children. Nonetheless, the only way he could become eligible to marry Anne of Brittany was to obtain an annulment of his marriage to Jeanne from Pope Alexander VI.

The Roman pontiff, knowing how badly Louis wished to add the duchy of Brittany to his domain, was in a position to drive a hard bargain. In exchange for granting a marriage annulment, Pope Alexander sought many favors on behalf of Cesare Borgia. The elder Borgia was grooming his illegitimate son to become a secular prince in his own right, and as a first step toward achieving this goal he persuaded Louis to invest Cesare with the counties of Valentinois and Diois in the summer of 1498. Since the former county was raised to the status of a duchy in the course of the negotiations, Cesare thereupon acquired the formal title of duke. Besides this, an annual pension of 20,000 francs was bestowed upon him, and a company of 100 French lancers was placed at his disposal for service in Italy or elsewhere. Even though Pope Alexander drew up an annulment decree at the end of the summer, it was not made public until the middle of December. On the very next day after the pro forma ecclesiastical tribune that was being held in Tours ended its inquiry, Cesare presented the papal decree to the French monarch at his royal palace in Chinon, a small town located several hundred miles southwest of Paris on the Vienne River. The marriage between Louis and Anne was subsequently celebrated in the castle of Nantes on 6 January 1499. As for Jeanne, the former duchess of Orléans went on to found a cloistered order once her marriage to Louis had been declared invalid. Because of this pious act, she was canonized shortly after her death in 1505.

The purpose of Cesare's trip to the royal court at Chinon was by no means limited to the presentation of a papal dispensation for the French monarch's divorce and remarriage; the emissary from Rome had matrimonial ambitions of his own. Cesare was, in fact, intent on marrying a daughter of King Federigo of Naples by the name of Carlotta, a young woman who happened to be serving as a maid of honor to Anne of Brittany at the time. Federigo was strongly opposed to a marital union between his daughter and a member of the Borgia family, and Cesare was fully aware that he needed the intercession of Louis and Anne if he were ever to obtain Carlotta's consent. Despite all the efforts made on Cesare's behalf by the royal couple, Carlotta refused to be persuaded. It was soon discovered that the perplexing behavior of the Neapolitan prin-

Louis XII: The Hereditary Prince

cess had a simple explanation: namely, she was already in love with a young Breton nobleman who was a member of Anne's royal retinue. Louis thereupon searched frantically for another bride who would be an acceptable substitute for Carlotta and eventually found one in the person of Charlotte d'Albret, a sister of the king of Navarre. She and Cesare were married at Blois on 12 May 1499. Despite his genuine affection for Charlotte, Cesare did not take her with him when he returned to Italy three months later and was destined never to see her again. Nor would he ever see the daughter with whom she was already pregnant when he took his leave from France. Even though Charlotte was only 25 years old at the time of his death on 12 March 1507 while employed as a mercenary in the service of her brother, this beautiful and wealthy woman went into mourning for the rest of her life.

At the time of his coronation on 27 May 1498, Louis had himself proclaimed king of Naples and Jerusalem as well as king of France. Because his grandmother had been a member of the Visconti family, he was likewise crowned duke of Milan. Obsessed with an ambition to incorporate the duchy of Milan into his royal domain, Louis was highly desirous of getting Cesare Borgia to participate in the upcoming campaign to unseat Lodovico Sforza as its ruler. Cesare, for his part, had political ambitions involving the territory of Romagna whose success depended on his receiving military support from the French monarch. The two men, consequently, entered into a pact of mutual aid. Cesare fulfilled his obligation to Louis by assuming command of a squadron of heavy cavalry in operations against the Milanese forces. The campaign turned out to be remarkably brief, and Louis rode into Milan in triumph on 6 October 1499. Lodovico had chosen to abandon his capital city as soon as the fortresses guarding the borders of the duchy fell into the hands of the French king and his Venetian allies. With Cesare's part of the agreement fulfilled, Louis reciprocated by supplying his Italian ally with an army composed of 1,800 French cavalry and more than 4,000 Swiss and Gascon infantry to be used in reasserting papal authority in the territories of Romagna and adjacent regions. Cesare's military ventures soon proved so successful that his father named him duke of Romagna in 1501. The newly appointed duke subsequently participated in the campaign against Naples that Louis undertook in conjunction with King Ferdinand of Aragon. The French and Spanish armies quickly overwhelmed their Neapolitan adversaries but quarreled with each other over the division of the spoils. After suffering several defeats at the hands of the Spaniards, Louis was forced to accept the fact that his territorial ambitions toward the Kingdom of Naples were nothing but illusory goals and had best be written off once and for all. He continued to interfere, however, in the military and political affairs of northern Italy until his death in 1515. All these endeavors likewise came to naught, and Louis left France no richer in territory despite all the men and money he had expended to increase the size of his domain.

Machiavelli believed that it is normal and natural for a prince to wish to gain control over new areas, but that Louis committed several major errors in his attempt to augment his domain by annexing territory in Italy. In the indictment of the policies pursued by the French monarch that appears in chapter 3, Machiavelli asserts: "So far, then, Louis had made these five mistakes: he had destroyed the lesser powers, had increased in Italy the might of one already great, had brought into the country a foreigner of great strength, had not come there to live, and had not brought in colonies" (1:19). The lesser powers that were destroyed are never identified by Machiavelli, but it is most likely that he is referring to Mantua, Ferrara, and Bologna, as well as to the city-states of Romagna that were subdued by Cesare Borgia with the support of French forces. The Italian power whose might was increased through the ventures initiated by the king of France is clearly identified as that of the papacy under Alexander VI, and the foreigner of great strength who intruded upon Italy is a reference to Ferdinand II of Aragon. As for the advisability of a ruler residing in an annexed territory and bringing in colonists from his homeland, it is well to remember that Louis was attempting to create a "mixed" principality. As defined by Machiavelli, a state of this type is one in which newly acquired territories are incorporated into the domain of a

Louis XII: The Hereditary Prince

hereditary ruler. Such a state had been created when the French monarchy absorbed the duchy of Brittany into its realm. But if the territory acquired differs in language, customs, and institutions from the hereditary principality, Machiavelli strongly urges the new ruler to live among his new subjects (as the Turks did in Greece) or send colonists into a few key areas of the new province (as the Romans did throughout the empire). Accordingly, Louis's failure to do either was one of the main reasons he was unable to retain control over the duchy of Milan in the long run.

Machiavelli then extends the scope of his indictment of the French monarch by asserting that Louis committed an error far more grievous than any of those cited above: "Even these mistakes, during his lifetime, might not have injured him if he had not made a sixth mistake, that of taking their dominion from the Venetians" (1:19). Machiavelli is referring to the 1509 French incursion into the territory of the Venetian republic, an act of naked aggression that lacked any legal justification whatsoever. Ironically, Venice had been a staunch military ally of France during the earlier conquest of Milan. Louis initially enjoyed the full support of Spain, Germany, and the papacy in his campaign against the Venetians. But these powers soon became alarmed at the overwhelming victories that were being achieved by the force of French arms, and they abruptly reversed their policy of support.

Foremost among the adversaries of the French monarch was Julius II. In 1511 this warrior-pope formed an alliance known as the Holy League—which included Venice, Spain, Germany, and England among its members—for the purpose of opposing the expansion of French power. On 11 April 1512 the troops of the Holy League and a French army under Gaston de Foix met on a field of battle in the vicinity of Ravenna. The French were to triumph decisively over the forces of the Holy League on that day, but their victory proved to be Pyrrhic. They not only suffered heavy casualties in the bloody battle, but their dashing commander—a courtly youth of 22—died with 16 separate wounds spread over his battered body. It was only a year later that Swiss allies of Pope Julius threatened to overrun the duchy of Milan. The only realistic expedient left to Louis was to abandon Milan as well as most other regions of Italy that were occupied by his troops. Despite all these reverses, he was still planning yet another invasion of Italy to recover the lost territories at the time of his death two years later. By then, French intervention in Italian affairs had become a habit and his successor, Francis I, continued to pursue this delusory course of action for several more decades.

In chapter 3 Machiavelli sets forth succinctly the lesson to be learned from Louis's misadventures in Italy: "From this we get a general rule that never or seldom deceives us: namely, he who is the reason for another's growing powerful falls; because he creates that power either with ingenuity or with force, and both of these are feared by the one who has grown powerful" (1:20). Thus, Louis's primary mistake was to increase the secular power of the papacy by assisting it in reasserting control over Romagna and adjacent regions. Machiavelli had the pleasure of communicating this conviction directly to the French themselves on the first of his four diplomatic missions to the court of King Louis as an emissary of Florence. On this occasion the man he chose to share his feelings with was Georges d'Amboise, cardinal of Rouen. This close adviser to the French monarch had been elevated from the rank of archbishop to that of cardinal in the autumn of 1499 as one of the conditions in the agreement through which Pope Alexander granted King Louis a dispensation to marry Anne of Brittany in exchange for the favors bestowed on his son. He subsequently proved to be Cesare Borgia's staunchest ally at the royal court. When Machiavelli argued that it was folly for the French to have actually honored their commitment to support Cesare's cause in Romagna militarily, the cardinal took issue with the Florentine secretary's remarks. Machiavelli sums up the incident as follows:

> On this subject I talked with Rouen at Nantes, when Valentino (for that was the popular name for Cesare Borgia, Pope Alexander's son) was taking over Romagna. For the reasons I have given, when the Cardinal of Rouen said to me that the Italians know nothing of war, I answered that the French know nothing of politics, because if they knew anything, they would not let the Church attain such strength. And ex-

Louis XII: The Hereditary Prince

perience shows that her strength in Italy, and that of Spain, have been caused by the King of France, and his ruin caused by them. (1:20)

Anyone whose knowledge of Louis XII is limited to the information purveyed in *The Prince* and other works by Machiavelli will be surprised to learn that his reign in toto has been assessed most positively by French historians, and that he is frequently referred to as "the father of the people" because of his honest endeavor to rule with justice and moderation.

Cesare Borgia 1475–1507. Portrait by Cristofano dell' Altissimo. Courtesy of the Uffizi Gallery, Florence.

7

Cesare Borgia: The New Prince

Far more challenging than the establishment by a hereditary ruler of a mixed principality is the task that faces an individual from the private sector who endeavors to become a new prince with a domain of his own. Not surprisingly, the new prince whose career Machiavelli scrutinizes most closely is that of Cesare Borgia. It was, in fact, the personal contact between Cesare and Machiavelli in 1502 and 1503 that informed the image of the ideal ruler that the latter would delineate in *The Prince*. Cesare's career, however, is inseparable from that of his father and needs to be examined within the context of the role that the Borgia family played in Italian history.

The Borgia family was of mixed Spanish and Catalonian ancestry and enjoyed the status of nobility within the kingdom of Aragon. The first member of the family to become a factor in Italian politics was Alonso de Borja (who subsequently Italianized his name to Alfonso Borgia). This canon lawyer, because of services rendered to both the crown and the Church, rose to become bishop of Valencia in 1429 and cardinal in 1444. Thereupon, at the age of 80, he was elevated to the papacy after the 1455 death of Nicholas V when a deadlocked conclave decided to select him as a compromise candidate. He had long expected, however, to become pope because the Spanish Dominican friar Vincent

Ferrer, whom he later canonized during the first year of his pontificate, had prophesied nearly a half-century earlier that he would one day occupy the Chair of Peter. It was assumed that a man of his age would be no more than a caretaker pontiff. Nonetheless, under the name of Calixtus III, this austere and pious churchman surprised everyone by proposing a crusade to reconquer Constantinople from the Turks, who had taken the city in 1453, and by working on behalf of this unconsummated project with enormous zeal throughout his three-year reign. He also did all in his power to advance the personal fortunes of his relatives and compatriots by conferring various ecclesiastical and secular offices on them whenever the opportunity to do so presented itself. Such acts of unabashed favoritism by the Spanish pontiff were deeply resented, and upon his death in 1458 the "Catalans" (as these papal appointees were known) had to run for their lives to escape the unleashed fury of the Roman populace.

Among the beneficiaries of Calixtus's nepotism were his nephews Luis Juan de Mila and Rodrigo Lanzol y Borja, both of whom were elevated to the rank of cardinal in the early part of 1456. Rodrigo, who had already Italianized his surname to Borgia, was only 26 at the time. The following year he also became the highest ranking administrative official at the Vatican when he was appointed vice-chancellor of the Church. Among other lucrative benefices that were bestowed on him was that of archbishop of Valencia. His great diplomatic and administrative skills, moreover, enabled him to retain all of these positions even after the anti-Catalan riots that followed the death of his uncle. His power actually increased under the next four pontiffs, and he finally managed to get elected to the papacy itself by purchasing the votes of many of the cardinals who took part in the conclave that was convened to choose a successor to Innocent VIII. He was 60 at the time of his election in 1492, and his reign under the name of Alexander VI was to continue for the next 11 years. His contemporaries accused him of venality, licentiousness, simony, theft, incest, and murder, and even today it is difficult for historians to separate fact from fiction in many of the allegations leveled against him. There can be no doubt, however, that his reputation for venality and and licentiousness was fully merited. In his early forties he had amassed a huge personal fortune by exploiting the prerogatives vested in his ecclesi-

Cesare Borgia: The New Prince

astical appointments for material gain. Throughout his entire career as a churchman, moreover, he made little attempt to conceal his strong sexual appetite. It has now been established that he sired nine or ten illegitimate children in relationships with various mistresses over the course of his lifetime. The mistress he had the longest relationship with was Vannozza Cattanei. Alexander finally cast aside this upright woman, with whom he conducted an affair for over 20 years, when he became enamored of a beautiful young woman 40 years his junior named Giulia Farnese. Known as *la Bella,* she became the mother of the pope's last three children.

Along with his passion for women and money, Alexander was also deeply committed to the aggrandizement of his relatives. Of special concern to him were the careers of the four children borne by his mistress Vannozza: Cesare, Giovanni (Juan), Lucrezia, and Goffredo (Jofré). Cesare, born in 1475, was destined for the Church and began to receive appointments to various ecclesiastical offices from the age of seven onward. In keeping with the spirit of the age, he received intensive instruction in the Greek and Roman classics during his childhood. Later, at age 14, he attended the university at Perugia, where he studied both canon and civil law, and after two years he decided to continue his studies in the Florentine city of Pisa largely for the sake of establishing social contacts with the Medici family. On 20 September 1493, at age 17, his father elevated him to the cardinalate along with Alessandro Farnese (a brother of his mistress Giulia as well as a future pope in his own right).

Giovanni, only one year younger than Cesare, was Pope Alexander's favorite son. It was he whom his father relied on to establish a secular Borgia dynasty. At 20 years of age Giovanni was made captain general of the papal army, duke of Benevento, and lord of Terracina. In addition, his father had earlier arranged for him to become ruler of the Aragonese duchy of Gandia and to marry a princess from the Spanish royal family.

Alexander similarly set up a series of brilliant marriages for Lucrezia. She first wed Giovanni Sforza of Pesaro at age 13 because of his connections with the rulers of Milan, but her father had the marriage annuled on the grounds of alleged impotency four years later when he decided to strengthen ties with Naples. He thereupon had her marry Duke Alfonso of Biscegle, an illegitimate son of the late king of Naples. This marriage likewise proved to be politically inconvenient owing to the newly resuscitated French claims to the southern kingdom being pressed by Louis XII, and it was deemed best to remove Duke Alfonso from the scene. Consequently, he was murdered at Rome with the complicity of Cesare Borgia himself in 1500. A year later, for the sake of strengthening the papacy's position in northern Italy, Lucrezia was wed to Alfonso d'Este, a widower who was the heir of the reigning duke of Ferrara. Lucrezia's subsequent deportment as duchess of Ferrara proved to be exemplary in all respects despite the scandalous reputation that she had acquired earlier in life. Among other things, it was widely believed that she had committed incest with her father and both of her elder brothers. Modern historians discount such allegations and have largely absolved her of any major moral transgressions whatsoever.

Goffredo, the youngest of the four siblings, married Sancia, an illegitimate daughter of Duke Alfonso of Calabria, when he was barely 13 years of age. The marriage took place by proxy at Rome in 1493 and was celebrated in Naples less than a year later. Goffredo received the rich territory of Squillace as part of his dowry and was content to reign as its prince for the rest of his life. Alexander was thus able to enhance his influence in southern Italy through this arrangement.

Cesare was never able to reconcile himself to the ecclesiastical career his father had selected for him. The unexpected demise of his brother Giovanni—an event that completely disrupted Alexander's plans to establish a secular dynasty for the Borgia family—presented him with an opportunity to free himself from this uncongenial calling.

On the evening of 14 June 1497 the two brothers had dined at the country home of their mother. Upon returning to Rome, they parted company when Giovanni excused himself to keep an urgent appointment. When he failed to return to his quarters at the Vatican by the following afternoon, Pope Alexander became alarmed and ordered that a search be made for his missing son. Early the next day a boatman reported that on the night of Giovanni's disappearance he had seen a group of men, one of whom was mounted on a white horse, approach the shoreline and toss a body into the Tiber River—a sight that he did not regard as unusual. On the basis of this information, Giovanni's body was recovered from the river later that same day, and a total of nine stab wounds were counted on his corpse. Despite his profound grief, the pontiff himself directed the search for the killers. But he abruptly called a halt to the investigation before even a full week had passed, and it was generally assumed that the identity of the guilty party had been discovered. Thereupon, to everyone's surprise, nothing further occurred, and the entire affair was left unresolved.

Eight months later, in February 1498, a rumor surfaced within diplomatic circles at Venice that it was Cesare himself who bore responsibility for Giovanni's murder, and this allegation gained increasing currency throughout Italy over the next few years. It must be stressed, however, that the evidence implicating him was purely circumstantial. The fact that the investigation had been suspended so quickly was taken as a clear indication that only the culpability of someone as close to the pontiff as his own son could have induced him to take such a drastic action. It was Cesare, moreover, who eventually profited the most by his brother's death. In August 1499 he formally requested that his appointment as cardinal be nullified on the grounds that his illegitimate birth disqualified him from holding such an exalted ecclesiastical office. In exchange for renouncing his cardinal's hat, Cesare was able to assume all of the prerogatives formally exercised by his late brother with one major exception. Owing to pressure exerted by Ferdinand and Isabella of Spain, the Aragonese duchy of Gandia was bestowed on Giovanni's only son.

Of course, Cesare was compensated for the loss of Gandia in full measure when he was subsequently made count, and later duke, of Valentinois as part of the agreement between his father and Louis XII annulling the French monarch's marriage to Jeanne of Valois. Because of his official rank as duke of Valentinois, Cesare soon came to be called Valentino. (Coincidentally, Calixtus III had also been nicknamed *il Valentino* from the time he took up residence at Rome in 1445 as a newly appointed cardinal from the bishopric of Valencia.) Late in the autumn of 1499, with troops supplied by Louis XII and funded by his father, Cesare moved into Romagna to evict the insubordinate vicars of the Holy See from the city-states under their control. In keeping with his recently acquired secular ambitions, he carried a sword decorated with engravings that depicted scenes from the life of Julius Caesar. Two mottoes were inscribed on the sword: on one side it read "Either Caesar or nobody" (*Aut Caesar aut nullus*), and on the other, "The die is cast" (*Alea iactus est*).

Cesare's first target was Caterina Sforza, a widow who had taken over control of the principalities of Imola and Forlì after her husband's assassination in 1488. Imola fell scarcely three weeks after Cesare had set forth from Milan, and Forlì was taken shortly thereafter. Caterina herself, however, continued to resist by taking refuge in Forlì's citadel, and it required a full month before Cesare's forces succeeded in breaching its defenses and taking her captive. Rumors were rife at the time that she had been raped by Cesare before being sent on to Rome for imprisonment. A little over a year later, upon agreeing to renounce all claims to her former territories, she was released through the intercession of the French.

After conquering Imola and Fiorlì, Cesare was compelled to halt his advance into Romagna when French military support was suddenly withdrawn. King Louis urgently needed the troops he had made available to Cesare for deployment against the forces of Lodovico Sforza, who had unexpectedly returned from exile in Germany and swiftly recaptured his native city, to the great joy of its citizenry. Machiavelli attributes the surprising ease with which Lodovico retook Milan to the French monarch's political ineptitude in governing an occupied city within an alien land. While Louis was engaged in retaking the city of Milan, Cesare turned over the administration of the territories under his control in Romagna to the Spaniard Ramiro de Lorqua and returned to Rome to participate in the festivities for the jubilee year of 1500.

During this sojourn in Rome, Cesare spent much of his time in the pursuit of sensual pleasures. Oddly enough, he even staged a Spanish-style bullfight in order to publicly exhibit his physical agility and spontaneous valor. Cesare also managed to enhance his reputation for ruthlessness when he came under suspicion of having hired the assassins who, one night in mid-August, broke into an apartment at the Vatican and strangled the Neapolitan spouse of his sister Lucrezia. Meanwhile, he succeeded in assembling an army composed of 10,000 Spanish, Italian,

Cesare Borgia: The New Prince

Gascon, and Swiss mercenaries under the leadership of professional military commanders known as *condottieri*. Among the *condottieri* who flocked to support his cause were many young Romans of aristocratic lineage such as Paolo and Carlo Orsini.

Cesare left Rome at the beginning of October and resumed his conquest of Romagna. By the end of the month his troops had already captured Pesara and Rimini, and he then moved on to Faenza. Its courageous citizens refused to surrender, however, and Cesare was compelled to lay siege to the city. It was not until 25 April 1501 that the defenders of Faenza agreed to capitulate. Soon thereafter, in recognition of his son's military exploits, Alexander named him duke of Romagna. At about the same time his father instructed him to return to Rome; Louis XII was already assembling his forces outside the walls of the city in preparation for the long-awaited invasion of Naples, and Cesare was obliged to honor his pledge to take part in that campaign. On the way back to Rome, he diverted his forces to the Sienese city of Piombino in an attempt to capture it for the papacy but was not on hand to accept its actual surrender several months later. He himself reached Rome on 13 June 1501.

Cesare left Rome approximately one month later at the head of a unit of 400 infantrymen from Romagna. The only serious resistance to the French advance was met about 40 miles north of Naples at the city of Capua. Once inside its gates, the invaders cast off all restraint and indulged in an orgy of pillage and rapine of unprecedented ferocity. At the end of three days more than 4,000 noncombatants had lost their lives and little remained of the city but a heap of smoldering ruins. Later accounts of this incident allege that Cesare locked the women of Capua in a tower and then chose 40 of the most beautiful to gratify his sexual desires. Modern historians, however, tend to dismiss this report as a malicious invention concocted by enemies of the Borgias. Be that as it may, the fall of Capua was soon followed by that of Naples itself, and Cesare was among the vanguard of Louis's army that entered the city on 3 August. Now having fulfilled his obligation to the French monarch, he returned to Rome in the middle of August and remained there for the next nine months.

Much of his time there was devoted to the recruitment and training of another army of his own, for Cesare was determined to free himself from dependence on troops provided by the French king. After assembling a powerful army of 6,000 infantry and 2,000 cavalry, he was ready to move against new targets in Romagna. When his forces left Rome on 10 June 1502, it was generally assumed that he intended to attack Camerino and Sinigallia. To everyone's surprise, however, Cesare chose to invade the duchy of Urbino and oust Guidobaldo da Montefeltro from his patrimony. There was, it must be stressed, no reason whatsoever for this loyal vicar of the Church to suspect that an attack on him might be launched by the pope's own son. Caught off guard by this act of treachery, he was obliged to abandon his palace in great haste during the night of 20 June to avoid falling into the hands of the invaders. Cesare and his forces entered Urbino the next morning, and he then declared himself duke of Urbino. His headquarters were located in the same ducal palace that was to serve as the setting for the dialogues that Baldassare Castiglione transcribed in his renowned treatise, *The Book of the Courtier*. It was also here, precisely one month after he had entered Urbino, that Cesare received the news of Camerino's surrender to the forces to which he had delegated the task of capturing that city.

Immediately prior to his march on Urbino, Cesare had sent word to the *Signoria* in Florence that he would like to enter into discussions with them on matters of mutual concern. The most pressing problem at the time was the status of Arezzo. Earlier that month its citizens rebelled against their Florentine overlords and sought political independence. Assisting the Aretines was one of Cesare's *condottieri* by the name of Vitellozzo Vitelli. This artillery expert from the Romagnol principality of Città di Castello harbored a consuming hatred toward the Florentines ever since they hanged his brother Paolo for bungling an attack on the city of Pisa while serving them as a *condottiere*. It is still unclear whether Vitellozzo acted on his own authority when he intervened in Arezzo or on orders from Cesare. The emissary selected by the Council of Ten for War to negotiate with Cesare was Francesco Soderini, the bishop of Volterra and brother of the recently elected gonfalonier for life. To assist Soderini, the council arranged for Niccolò Machiavelli to accompany him. It took only two days for the two men to complete the journey from

Cesare Borgia: The New Prince

Florence to Urbino, and immediately upon their arrival they were summoned into the presence of their host.

That Cesare made a favorable impression on Machiavelli from the very outset is amply attested to by the letter that he sent back to his superiors on 26 June 1502:

> This prince is very splendid and magnificent, and in war he is so bold that there is no great enterprise that does not seem small to him, and to gain glory and territory he never rests or knows danger or weariness: he arrives at a place before anyone has heard that he has left the place he was in before: he wins the love of his soldiers, and has got hold of the best men in Italy. These things make him victorious and formidable, and are attended with invariable good fortune. (Ridolfi, 50)

There is evidence that Duke Valentino likewise held Machiavelli in high esteem. The secretary readily obtained audiences with Cesare, and the length of these sessions indicated that the lord of Romagna truly enjoyed his company. Although Soderini remained in Urbino for five full weeks, Machiavelli returned to Florence after only a few days to give the *Signoria* an oral briefing on Cesare's intentions. Diplomatic pressure applied by the French monarch soon compelled Cesare to withdraw his forces from Tuscan territory. During the next few months, Machiavelli undertook other diplomatic missions on behalf of the Council of Ten for War, including three visits to Arezzo.

In the meantime Cesare engaged in diplomatic activities of his own. Toward the end of July he left Urbino disguised as a knight of St. John of Jerusalem with only four attendants and journeyed north to the court of King Louis at Milan. Once there, he not only managed to alleviate the tensions between the French monarch and himself that had arisen because of Vitellozzo's harassment of the Florentines, but also succeeded in negotiating a treaty that granted him additional military aid for his campaign in Romagna. Cesare's plans for further conquests were to receive a serious setback, however. His recent successes at Urbino and Camerino had caused much unrest and insecurity within the ruling circles of such principalities as Perugia, Bologna, and Città di Castello, which were located within the States of the Church. Fear had also spread among many of his own military commanders. Perhaps at the instigation of the ruler of neighboring Siena, many of the concerned parties met at the castle of La Magione near Perugia during October and entered into a conspiracy to eliminate the threat that Cesare posed to their lives and to the states they controlled. The citizens of Urbino took immediate advantage of the confused state of affairs by ousting Cesare's henchmen and recalling Duke Guidobaldo. The Florentines dispatched Machiavelli to Cesare's headquarters at Imola to obtain an accurate assessment of the military situation; he would remain in personal contact with Cesare from 7 October 1502 to 18 January 1503.

Machiavelli was immensely impressed by Cesare's composure during this period of crisis in his personal fortunes and soon became convinced that his adversaries would not prevail. On 23 October 1502, just two weeks after his arrival at Imola, he summed up the situation for the benefit of his superiors back in Florence: "As to the state of things here, the government of this Lord since I have been here has rested only on his good fortune—the cause of which has been the firm opinion commonly held that the King of France would aid him with soldiers, and the Pope with money; then there is another thing that has worked for him no less than this one, namely, the sluggishness of his enemies in pressing him" (1:128). He also asserted that, in his judgment, it was too late for anyone to inflict serious harm on Cesare, for the duke had already provided all the important cities with garrisons and all the fortresses with provisions.

Despite some initial successes by troops under their command, Cesare's foes apparently reached the same conclusion. Seizing the moment, Cesare suppressed his desire to avenge himself against the renegade commanders for the time being and offered to enter into negotiations with them. The offer was readily accepted. As part of the settlement reached between the two parties, Cesare's erstwhile confederates agreed to retake Urbino and other cities in his name. On 10 December Cesare moved his headquarters from Imola to Cesena and remained there for the next 16 days. While at Cesena he decided to resolve a long-standing problem that had been undermining his rule in the region. Ramiro de Lorqua, the man whom he had appointed to serve as military governor of

Cesare Borgia: The New Prince

Romagna nearly two years earlier, had come to be intensely hated by the inhabitants of the territories that he administered owing to his sadistic temperament and heinous acts of cruelty. On the morning of Cesare's departure, Lorqua's decapitated corpse was discovered lying in the main piazza alongside a bloodstained sword. The head was mounted on a pike for all to inspect. In his official report dated 26 December 1502, Machiavelli relates that Lorqua "this morning was found in two pieces on the public square, where he still is; and all the people have been able to see him. Nobody feels sure of the cause of his death, except that so it has pleased the Prince, who shows that he can make and unmake men as he likes, according to their deserts" (1:142).

On the same day that Cesare had Lorqua dispatched, Sinigallia was captured on his behalf by some of the *condottieri* who had been key members of the conspiracy against him and were now ostensibly attempting to demonstrate their loyalty to his cause. Cesare received news of the city's surrender two days later while at Fano. He was told that there was a complicating factor: namely, the citadel of Sinigallia continued to hold out because its castellan, Andrea Doria, refused to surrender to anyone other than himself. Cesare immediately suspected that the problem over the citadel's surrender was a stratagem in a plot devised by the *condottieri* to entrap him. Cesare agreed to go to Sinigallia, but he was determined to strike first. On the morning of 31 December 1502 he met with the disloyal *condottieri* on the outskirts of Sinigallia and insisted that they withdraw all their troops from the city so that the men in his own forces could be quartered there. This having been accomplished, he then persuaded the four leading conspirators to accompany him into the palace that had been selected to serve as his headquarters so that he might consult with them over weighty matters of state. Once inside, all four were immediately seized. Vitellozzo Vitelli and Oliverotto da Fermo were thereupon strangled by Michelotto da Corella, a man of Spanish origin who frequently served as Cesare's executioner. In contrast to Oliverotto, who died badly, Vitellozzo maintained his dignity to the very end. His sole request was that the pope be petitioned to grant him a plenary indulgence for all his sins. The other two men—Paolo Orsini and his cousin Francesco, the duke of Gravina—were spared for the time being.

Nonetheless, they too were strangled before another month had passed once Cesare realized that there was no profit to be gained by holding them hostage any longer.

Machiavelli did not arrive in Sinigallia until many hours after the four *condottieri* had been seized and hence was not an actual eyewitness to the events of the day. He did, however, receive a detailed accounting from Cesare himself that very night. By that time the castellan of the citadel had fled in panic. Machiavelli truly relished the manner in which "a most beautiful deception" had been carried out and shortly thereafter wrote a highly laudatory analysis of Cesare's activities at Sinigallia, "A Description of the Method Used by Duke Valentino in Killing Vitellozzo Vitelli, Oliverotto da Fermo, Sir Paolo, and the Duke of Gravina Orsini" (*Descrizione del modo tenuto dal Duca Valentino nell' ammazzare Vitellozzo Vitelli, Oliverotto da Fermo, il signor Pagolo, e il Duca di Gravina Orsini*). Another man who shared Machiavelli's admiration for the way the *condottieri* were dealt with at Sinigallia was none other than King Louis himself. Upon hearing of the incident, he is said to have proclaimed Cesare's deed to be worthy of a Roman hero.

Cesare, accompanied by Machiavelli, left Sinigallia on 1 January 1503. His next objective was to expel Pandolfo Petrucci from Siena, since it was Petrucci who had apparently masterminded the conspiracy of the *condottieri* from the outset. This goal was achieved by the end of the month, and Cesare's triumph was now complete. Machiavelli was not present at the surrender of Siena; he and the duke had parted company approximately two weeks earlier when the Florentines decided to recall their emissary. Cesare spent the next six months consolidating his control over Romagna and, in the process, did much to foster political reform and economic development in the region. Then, suddenly, both he and his father were taken ill in August with what now appears to have been malaria. Alexander died after a few days, but his son managed to survive. By the time Cesare was fully recovered, there was already a new pope, Pius III. Sixty-four at the time of his elevation, he died in less than a month. While Pius III did confirm Cesare in his position as papal vicar of Romagna, the duke was deprived of all of his conquests except Forlì, Imola, Cesena, and Faenza. When Machiavelli was dispatched to Rome at

Cesare Borgia: The New Prince

the end of October to act as a diplomatic observer at the conclave that was convened to elect a successor to the late Pius III, he was told by Cesare himself that all his current difficulties were to be attributed to the extremely malignant workings of fortune. In chapter 7 Machiavelli reports that Cesare told him "he had imagined what could happen when his father died, and for everything he had found a solution, except he had never imagined that at the time of that death he too would be close to dying" (1:33).

Since Cesare retained the loyalty of the large Spanish contingent in the College of Cardinals and could control their votes, whoever was to emerge victorious from the conclave sorely needed his support. One of the leading candidates was Giuliano della Rovere, a nephew of Pope Sixtus IV. It was Giuliano who had been Rodrigo Borgia's chief rival at the 1492 conclave held after the death of Innocent VIII, when Rodrigo had been elected pope. Because of the circumstances surrounding his loss, Giuliano became a bitter opponent of Alexander VI and did all in his power to nullify the result of the conclave. But his efforts to convene a church council to depose Pope Alexander for having gained his office through the commission of simony came to naught, and he was soon forced into exile in France. To win Cesare's support for his renewed candidacy in 1503, Giuliano promised to reconfirm him as papal vicar in Romagna. To Machiavelli's utter bewilderment, Cesare thereupon agreed to throw his support behind the candidacy of Giuliano, and as a result, his erstwhile enemy was elevated to the papacy under the name of Julius II. But before long it became obvious that His Holiness had no intention of honoring the commitment he had made to Cesare.

From Machiavelli's vantage point, Cesare's failure to support an alternative candidate at this time was the sole error in his entire political career. In chapter 7 Machiavelli emphatically declares:

> The single thing for which we can blame him is the election of Julius as pope. In this he made a bad choice because, as I have said, if he could not set up a pope himself, he could exclude from the papacy whomever he wished. He should never have let the papacy go to any cardinal whom he had injured or who, on becoming pope, would need to fear

> him, because men do injury through either fear or hate. . . . To believe that new benefits make men of high rank forget old injuries is to deceive oneself. In this choice, then, the Duke blundered, and it caused his final ruin. (1:34)

By the summer of 1504 Cesare had been stripped of his last strongholds in Romagna. He was much too dangerous to be allowed to remain in Italy, however, and Pope Julius deemed it best to send him into Iberian exile. Less than three years later, Cesare was dead at the age of 31.

8

Five Roads To Power

In *The Prince* Machiavelli distinguishes five ways in which men may rise from a private station to rulership of a principality. First, there are those who do so by means of the exercise of their own *virtù*. Among the historical figures he singles out as men who manifested a superior degree of *virtù* are Moses, Cyrus, Romulus, and Theseus. He cites the career of Francesco Sforza as a contemporary example of the function of *virtù* in the acquisition and retention of a principality. Second, there are those men whose rise to power was due to special favors conferred by *fortuna*. To demonstrate the role that *fortuna* plays in political and military affairs, Machiavelli examines extensively Cesare Borgia's attempt to make himself duke of Romagna. Third, some become rulers by committing criminal deeds; he discusses Agathocles of Syracuse as an ancient example and Oliverotto da Fermo as a modern one. Fourth, some men come to power by the favor of their fellow citizens and establish what is often translated as a "civil principality." Machiavelli prefers to analyze this type of power in general terms but does make a few brief remarks about the career of Nabis of Sparta as a case in point. Fifth, there are those nonhereditary rulers who gain princedoms by being elevated to a religious office of high rank. Machiavelli classifies such territories as "ecclesiatical principalities" but, with obvious irony, declines to analyze them; as he explains in chapter 11, "since they are set on high and maintained by God, to discuss them would be the act of a man presumptuous and rash" (1:44). Instead, he prefers to focus on the policies pursued by Alexander VI and Julius II in their exercise of authority over the States of the Church.

Machiavelli actually has little to say about the *virtù* of Francesco Sforza other than to remark in chapter 7 that he "by the necessary methods and by means of his great ability [i.e., *virtù*], though born to a private station became Duke of Milan; and what with a thousand exertions he gained, with little effort he kept" (1:28). Francesco came from a family of *condottieri,* and it was his father, Muzio Attendolo, who acquired the cognomen Sforza—a name derived from the Italian word that means "to use force"—owing to his enormous physical and mental prowess. Francesco himself won military fame in the employ of various princes and states before becoming a *condottiere* in the service of the Milanese duke Filippo Maria Visconti, whose daughter Bianca Maria he married in 1443. When his father-in-law died without a male heir, Francesco assumed the title of duke of Milan and reigned as such from 1450 to 1466. He had 30 children, of whom 21 were born outside of wedlock. It was Lodovico, the second and ablest of his legitimate children, who eventually succeeded him as duke of Milan.

In chapter 20, it should be noted, Machiavelli tempers his earlier commendation of Francesco by taking him to task for attempting to enhance his personal security through the construction of a mighty fortress: "The conclusion, then, can be stated thus: a wise prince who is more afraid of his own people than of foreigners builds fortresses; he who is more afraid of foreigners than his own people rejects them. The Sforza family has been and will be more damaged by the castle of Milan, which Francesco Sforza built, than by any other bad policy in that state" (1:80). In the duke's defense, it may be argued that he was by no means as indifferent to the goodwill of his subjects as Machiavelli implies. Francesco was never capriciously cruel, and he did much to promote the economic and cultural welfare of the duchy. On one count, however, Machiavelli is correct: the castle did prove to be useless in the defense of Milan when Louis XII invaded the duchy in 1499. Lodovico left the fortified castle under the command of his most trusted lieutenant with instructions to hold it at all costs and then fled north to the court of Emperor Maximilian in Germany. All that was required of King Louis to take control of the castle was to pay that lieutenant the sum of 150,000 French ducats.

Nonetheless, in Machiavelli's eyes, Francesco Sforza remains a true exemplar of *virtù*. The precise meaning of this concept, however, remains elusive. The term is used 59 times in *The Prince* (exclusive of its adjectival and adverbial variants). It cannot usually be equated with the traditional notion of virtue, although many translators of *The Prince* have rendered it as such. More commonly, the word *virtù* is translated as ability, capability, capacity, competence, courage, efficacy, ingenuity, merit, power, quality, resource, strategy, talent, vigor, or worth, as the context may require. Whenever Machiavelli sets up an opposition between *virtù* and *fortuna*, as he frequently does, it is appropriate to translate *virtù* as either ability or ingenuity. It is, moreover, closely related to the Latin concept of *virtus*, which, like its Greek counterpart *arete*, signifies excellence. Unlike *arete*, however, the word *virtus* has strong masculine connotations owing to its derivation from *vir*—the Latin designation for an individual male. (The Romans used the terms *femina* and *mulier* to refer to individual females. The word *homō* could be used to designate a human being irrespective of gender.) In general, *virtù* is employed in *The Prince* to mean an exceptional capacity for the kind of action that brings success in military and civic affairs.

Perhaps the most graphic illustration of Machiavelli's concept of *virtù* is to be found in his recommendation that a ruler must know how to suppress his human nature and to assume the characteristics of a beast. In chapter 18 he urges princes to emulate the wiliness of a fox and the strength of a lion. The controversial nature of this advice lies in Machiavelli's emphasis on the deceptiveness of the fox and the brutality of the lion. The animal symbolism that Machiavelli employs in this context is by no means original with him and was apparently derived from Cicero's handbook about the nature of ethics, *On Moral Conduct* (*De officiis*). In chapter 13 of book 1, Cicero condemns the use of either fraud or force in human affairs and equates fraud with the fox and force with the lion. Although he censures both forms of behavior as wholly unworthy of man, he views fraud as the more contemptible owing to the element of hypocrisy that such conduct entails. Machiavelli, on the other hand, adopts Cicero's symbolism of the fox and the lion but completely reverses the moral status Cicero gives to fraud and violence. In his view, there are many times when it is entirely legitimate for a prince to deceive his adversaries and to employ violence against them. While Machiavelli neglects to name any historical personage who distinguished himself for his leonine qualities, the individual he singles out as the foremost practitioner of the art of deception is none other than Pope Alexander: "Alexander VI never did anything else and never dreamed of anything else than deceiving men, yet he always found a subject to work on. Never was there a man more effective in swearing and who with stronger oaths confirmed a promise, but yet honored it less. Nonetheless, his deceptions always prospered as he hoped, because he understood well this aspect of the world" (1:65). The art of deception has, of course, come to be closely identified with Machiavelli himself. The Roman emperor Tiberius, who ruled from A.D. 14 to 37, is often referred to as "the imperial Machiavelli" because of his political axiom, "He who knows not how to dissemble knows not how to reign."

If ever anyone combined the attributes of the fox and the lion, it certainly was Cesare Borgia. Machiavelli himself admits as much when, in chapter 6, he declares that "indeed I for my part do not see what better precepts I can give a new prince than the examples of Duke Valentino's actions." Yet, surprisingly, he prefers to view the duke's career exclusively from the perspective of the influence exerted by *fortuna* and asserts that Cesare "gained his position through his father's Fortune and through her lost it" (1:28–29).

The concept of *fortuna,* like *virtù,* is notoriously difficult to define. Essentially, it refers to the area of experience that lies entirely outside human control, an area that includes events for which no rational causes are detectable. The term may be derived from mythology: there are some fairly reliable indications that the Roman goddess Fortuna was first worshiped as an agricultural deity who governs all those factors outside the farmer's control. In time, however, she developed into a goddess of luck or chance, much like her Greek counterpart Tyche. The notion of *tychē* (chance), it should be noted, played an important role in Greek philosophy among such thinkers as Plato, Aristotle, and the atomists Leucippus and Democritus. Aristotle distinguishes *tychē* from *automaton,* a term he applies to purely spontaneous or accidental events that serve no discernible intention or goal. Machiavelli does not appear, however, to have adopted such a distinction. Unlike Aristotle, moreover, he chooses to personify the concept of chance as a goddess who takes pleasure in change for its own sake and fashions the destinies of men according to her whim. The degree to which he is capable of personifying the concept of chance is best seen in his "Tercets on Fortune," a poem of unknown date. Here, underscoring the capriciousness of this goddess, Machiavelli writes: "Not a thing in the world is eternal; Fortune wills it so and makes herself splendid by it, so that her power may be more clearly seen. / Therefore a man should take her for his star and, as far as he can, should every hour adjust himself to her variation" (2:748).

In chapter 25, however, Machiavelli makes it very clear that men are not totally at the mercy of the vagaries of *fortuna*. While conceding that it may be true that the goddess controls half of men's actions, he maintains that she allows them direction of the other half, or almost half. Even this ratio may be altered, moreover, in the lives of men whose character and conduct prove attractive to the goddess:

> I conclude then (with Fortune varying and men remaining stubborn in their ways) that men are successful while they are in close harmony with Fortune, and when they are out of harmony, they are unsuccessful. As for me, I believe this: it is better to be impetuous than cautious, because Fortune is a woman and it is necessary, in order to keep her under, to cuff and maul her. She more often lets herself be overcome by men using such methods than by those who proceed coldly; therefore always, like a woman, she is the friend of young men, because they are less cautious, more spirited, and with more boldness master her. (1:92)

In other words, the goddess Fortuna favors a man of *virtù*. In addition, many of the hazards posed by *fortuna* may be neutralized through the exercise of prudence. To underscore this point, Machiavelli likens *fortuna* to a river in flood whose ravages may be mitigated, or avoided altogether, if men have made provisions to contain it by building levees and dikes. On the other hand, it also takes a man of *virtù* to take full advantage of the opportunities offered by *fortuna*.

Machiavelli never formally examines the interplay between *virtù* and *fortuna* in any part of *The Prince*, even though the career of Cesare Borgia obviously might have provided him with a perfect occasion to do so. Anyone interested in such an analysis, however, need only consult *The Life of Castruccio Castracani* (*La vita di Castruccio Castracani*), a semifictional narrative dealing with the military exploits of a Florentine *condottiere* who flourished around 1300; Machiavelli wrote it in 1520 while on a visit to Lucca.

Of the two men Machiavelli discusses as examples of those who became princes through the commission of crimes, Agathocles of Syracuse constitutes a far more important historical figure than does Oliverotto da Fermo. Agathocles, a man of humble origin, was born in the coastal region of northern Sicily and migrated to Syracuse in his early youth. He pursued a career in the city's militia and distinguished himself in a series of local wars. In 317 B.C. Agathocles became tyrant of Syracuse by ousting the oligarchs who had been in charge. Agathocles lured three of his most prominent political adversaries to a meeting at one of the Syracuse civic centers on the pretext of discussing the advisability of dispatching military aid to one of their allies whose city was then under siege by hostile forces. The three men, accompanied by approximately 200 retainers, were promptly massacred with great ferocity. Agathocles, who had taken the military precaution of closing all the gates of the city to ensure that no one escaped, thereupon urged his soldiers and the citizenry of Syracuse to exterminate all of the 600 oligarchs who held seats in the governing assembly, as well as anyone suspected of being sympathetic toward them.

For those who have difficulty in distinguishing between the morality of the actions of Agathocles at Syracuse and those of Cesare Borgia at Sinigallia, Machiavelli hastens to point out the crucial difference: the degree of Agathocles' violence was clearly excessive in its scope and inhumanity. Machiavelli could have pointed out another difference: namely, that Cesare's attempt to seize control of Romagna was potentially a prelude to the expulsion of foreign powers from Italian soil and the reunification of Italy under his leadership. Even though much of Agathocles' subsequent military activity was directed against the Carthaginians, who were attempting to wrest control of Sicily from the Greek settlers, he fought only to enhance his own personal power and lacked any political vision that might have redeemed his proclivity to wanton cruelty. He did, however, manage to stay in power for almost three decades until his death in 289 B.C. at the age of 50.

In contrast to Agathocles' lengthy tenure as tyrant of Syracuse, Oliverotto's rule in the principality of Fermo lasted less than a year after he rose to power by murdering the maternal uncle who had raised him after the death of his parents. His own life ended abruptly at the age of 25 when Cesare Borgia had him strangled, along with Vitellozzo Vitelli, at Sinigallia on 31 December 1502.

While Machiavelli genuinely admires the military valor exhibited by Agathocles throughout his career, he nonetheless refuses to consider him a man of true *virtù* owing to his excessive cruelty and inhumanity. There is, Machiavelli contends, a prudent way for a prince to inflict injury. It is most important that a prince commit all acts of cruelty at one time, rather than piecemeal, so as to permit the resumption of normal life as soon as possible. Machiavelli justifies this principle in chapter 8 by arguing that "injuries are to be done all together, so that, being savored less, they will anger less," and conversely, "benefits are to be conferred little by little, so they will be savored more" (1:38). Ignoring his previous condemnation of the tyrant of Syracuse, Machiavelli asserts that it was precisely Agathocles' intuitive understanding of this principle that enabled him to exercise control over his subjects for such an extended period of time. This apparent contradiction in Machiavelli's argument may be reconciled by consulting the historical record. Despite the fact that Agathocles rose to power through the commission of a heinous act, all bloodshed within the city ceased as soon as his position was secure. Thereafter, most of his deeds of cruelty were inflicted on enemies in time of war. He did, to be sure, shed blood within the city of Syracuse from time to time, but such instances of his cruelty were relatively rare. For the most part, Agathocles behaved in a pleasant and conciliatory manner toward his subjects and had little difficulty in winning the goodwill of the vast majority of Syracusans.

The next type of new prince that Machiavelli discusses is the one who achieves office by the favor of his fellow citizens and thereby establishes a civil principality. Here, in chapter 9, he stresses how important it is for a ruler to have the support of his people and cites Nabis of Sparta as a case in point: "Nabis, Prince of the Spartans, withstood a siege by all Greece and by a Roman army flushed with victory, and against them defended his city and his own position; and when that danger came upon him he needed to do no more than secure himself against a few disloyal citizens, though if his people had been hostile, that would not have been enough" (1:41). This point is underscored in chapter 40 of book 1 of the *Discourses,* where Machiavelli argues the relative merits of the support of the people as opposed to that of the nobility in preserving a prince's rule; he asserts that if one cannot secure the support of both parties, it is preferable to have the people on one's side. "With the support of the people, internal forces are enough for preservation, as they were enough for Nabis, tyrant of Sparta; for when all Greece and the Roman people attacked him, he first made himself sure of a few nobles; then with the aid of a friendly populace he defended himself; yet he could not have done so if the people had been his enemies" (1:283).

It is generally assumed that Machiavelli's views on Nabis are based on the information in Livy's history of Rome. Oddly enough, however, Livy unequivocally asserts that the city of Sparta escaped capture on this occasion solely because of the courageous leadership of the commander of its military garrison—a close relative of Nabis by the name of Pythagoras. Machiavelli's remarks on Nabis are also misleading on several other counts. For one thing, it is inaccurate to imply that the citizens of Sparta selected Nabis to be their ruler. In reality, he seized power illegally in 207 B.C. when the young Spartan king, Pelops, died under highly suspicious circumstances in which Nabis himself may have been implicated. The defense of Sparta in 195 B.C. by Nabis and his forces was, moreover, far less successful than Machiavelli's comments would lead one to believe. While it is true that the Romans never actually occupied the city, Nabis was, in fact, compelled to capitulate to his enemies by agreeing to a truce that exacted many harsh concessions from the Spartans. As for Nabis himself, his reign of 14 years as tyrant of Sparta came to an end three years later when he was assassinated during a coup d'état in that city. All in all, the example of Nabis does very little to substantiate Machiavelli's analysis of civil principalities.

The rulers who enjoy the greatest security, Machiavelli firmly maintains, are those who preside over ecclesiastical principalities, since their stewardship of such territories is sanctioned by long-established religious traditions. No sooner having made this assertion, however, he proceeds to describe the chaotic situation that prevailed within the States of the Church prior to the reign of Alexander VI, when most of the papal vicars had rejected the authority vested in the Holy See and acted as though they were a law unto themselves. The city of Rome itself, moreover, had been turned into a permanent battleground owing to the internecine fight that raged between the Orsini and Colonna families for political and economic supremacy. Machiavelli cites the brevity of a pope's tenure in office—an average of ten years—as the chief reason the papal vicars and Roman barons were never subdued once and for all despite repeated attempts by some pontiffs to do so. Nonetheless, in chapter 11 he argues that Alexander was far more capable than his predecessors and showed "beyond all the pontiffs who ever reigned how mighty a pope could be in both money and arms" (1:45).

Among the measures taken by Alexander to which Machiavelli alludes was the confiscation of properties belonging to the Colonna family in 1495 after Prospero Colonna, who had been serving as a *condottiere* in the forces that Charles VIII deployed against the Kingdom of Naples, suddenly switched sides and allied himself with the Neapolitan king Ferrantino. The Orsini family was dealt its severest blow during the winter of 1502–03 when three of its members were put to death at approximately the same time. In suppressing the conspiracy of the *condottieri* at Sinigallia, Cesare Borgia had Vitellozzo Vitelli and Oliverotto da Fermo executed immediately but decided to keep Paolo Orsini and his cousin Francesco as prisoners for the moment. Most likely the lives of the two

Orsinis were spared on that night because they had a powerful protector back in Rome in the person of Cardinal Gianbattista Orsini. But Alexander moved swiftly upon hearing of the events that occurred at Sinigallia and had the cardinal as well as many other members of the Orsini family placed under arrest and imprisoned. Cardinal Orsini died in a dungeon located within Castel Sant' Angelo on 22 February 1503, and it was widely believed that he had been poisoned. When news of the cardinal's demise reached Cesare at Assisi, he immediately gave orders for the two Orsinis in his custody to be strangled. Even though most of the troublesome vicars of Romagna had also been removed by this time, the secular ambitions of both Cesare and his father came to an abrupt end when they were simultaneously stricken with malaria. Shortly after the death of Alexander, the Colonna and Orsini families returned to Rome and recovered much of their former status under the reigns of Julius II and Leo X. Nevertheless, the secular arm of the papacy had been so strengthened by the Borgias that these families were steadily reduced to a position of subservience to the Holy See within the next few decades. The feud between the two rival clans was officially terminated when Marcantonio Colonna married Felice Orsini in 1552.

Despite having been a lifelong enemy of the Borgias, Julius II found himself the beneficiary of their secular ventures upon his ascension to the Chair of Peter. Born Giuliano della Rovere, he was the nephew of Sixtus IV—the same pope who commissioned the building of the Sistine Chapel in 1473. Hence, it is most fitting that Julius was the one to employ the talents of Michelangelo to decorate the ceiling of this papal chapel from 1508 to 1512. It was also Julius who decided to demolish the old basilica of St. Peter, an edifice which dated back to the time of the Roman emperor Constantine the Great, and to replace it with a new structure on the same site, a task of monumental proportions that took from 1506 to 1626 to complete. Not to be overlooked is the decision he made in 1503 to issue the dispensation that enabled Henry VIII of England to marry his brother's widow, Catherine of Aragon.

Unlike most of his immediate predecessors, Julius was not concerned with the aggrandizement of his relatives. His primary interests lay in restoring and extending the territories belonging to the States of the

Five Roads to Power

Church as well as in expelling the French from Italian soil. His efforts in pursuit of these objectives, it should be noted, proved to be highly successful in all respects. The major crisis confronting Julius upon his elevation to the papacy stemmed from the Venetian attempt to annex the province of Romagna after Cesare Borgia had been deposed as its duke. It was to take several years, however, before he was able to bring this region fully under his control. Matters came to a climax in 1509 when Julius issued a papal bull placing the entire Adriatic republic under a ban of excommunication. A year later, with the help of military forces from France, Germany, and Spain, he compelled the Venetians to sign a peace treaty of the severest kind. Thereafter, Julius concentrated on expelling the French from Italy and succeeded in doing so by the end of his reign.

It must be stressed that Julius was no mere armchair military strategist. More of a warrior than a priest, he frequently took to the field of battle arrayed in full armor. One of the people who took a dim view of Julius's martial ardor was Desiderius Erasmus. This renowned Dutch humanist held that such bellicosity was wholly incompatible with the office of Holy Father. Although his name never appears in *The Praise of Folly* (*Moriae encomium*) (1511), it is clear that Erasmus's satirical comments about militant pontiffs are a direct attack on Pope Julius. Upon hearing the news of the pontiff's demise in 1513, Erasmus penned a vitriolic dialogue, *Julius Excluded from Paradise* (*Julius exclusus*), in which he relates how Julius is turned away from the gates of paradise after a heated argument with St. Peter.

Not sharing Erasmus's moral sentiments, Machiavelli takes a far more positive view of Pope Julius and his 10-year reign. Machiavelli had a firsthand opportunity to study the pontiff's character during Julius's campaign to reassert papal authority over the principalities of Perugia and Bologna. Julius personally led his forces out of Rome on 26 August 1506, and Machiavelli joined the pontiff's traveling court a day later in the capacity of an official observer for the Florentine republic. The secretary was to remain with the papal court until the middle of November, at which time he returned to Florence to be present at the birth of one of his children. Prior to his departure, however, he had witnessed the abject submission of the papal vicar in Perugia and the precipitous flight of his counterpart in Bologna. The image of Julius in *The Prince* is one of a person who unstintingly dedicated himself to the welfare of the papacy and to the cause of Italian sovereignty. In short, Machiavelli sees Julius as a man of *virtù*. This is a very generous assessment in view of the fact that it was Julius who restored the Medici to power in Florence and thus was responsible for the termination of Machiavelli's own career as a civil servant for the republic to whose political continuity he was so passionately committed.

9

Military Considerations

The role of military power in affairs of state is central to all of Machiavelli's political thought. In chapter 12 of *The Prince* he unequivocally asserts that "the principal foundations of all states, the new as well as the old and the mixed, are good laws and good armies. And because there cannot be good laws where armies are not good, and where there are good armies, there must be good laws, I shall omit talking of laws and speak of armies" (1:47). The importance Machiavelli attached to this proposition may be confirmed by the fact that he repeats it in the *Discourses*. In chapter 31 of book 3, he asserts: "Elsewhere I have said that the foundation of all states is good military organization, and that where this does not exist there cannot be good laws or anything else good, because at every point in reading Livy's *History* this certainly appears" (1:500). Much of the content of the *Discourses* is devoted to the interrelationship that existed between the Roman military organization and the Roman political constitution.

A few years after completing *The Prince* and the *Discourses*, Machiavelli published *The Art of War*. In the preface he reiterates by way of analogy his belief that civil institutions must rely on military force for security against foreign and domestic enemies: "And so . . . good customs, without military support, suffer the same sort of injury as do the rooms of a splendid and kingly palace, even though ornamented with gems and gold, when, not being roofed over, they have nothing to protect them from the rain" (2:566).

It was the political crisis precipitated by the French invasion of Italy by the troops of Charles VIII in 1494 that had raised questions of military strategy to a position of central importance for individuals like Machiavelli. Prior to this traumatic event, the type of warfare waged within the Italian peninsula during the fifteenth century had been a relatively bloodless affair. As the city-states of northern Italy had grown in wealth, they had found it expedient to entrust matters of defense to *condottieri* and the mercenary troops in their employ. These rootless military commanders and their troops were extremely loath to risk their own lives and tended to shun battle if at all possible. Cities were besieged rather than stormed, and military campaigns in the field usually involved more maneuver than combat. Casualties were also kept to a minimum by the *condottieri*'s preference for using cavalry over foot soldiers and artillery. Machiavelli devotes the entire twelfth chapter of *The Prince* to a vituperative attack on this military system and unequivocally declares that such mercenary troops are worthless because "they are disunited, ambitious, without discipline, disloyal; valiant among friends, among enemies cowardly; they have no fear of God, no loyalty to men" (1:47).

All these shortcomings were exposed in a dramatic fashion by the swift, easy victories scored by the French invaders and their Swiss and German auxiliaries. Whereas the Italian cavalry units were composed of mercenaries, those of the French were drawn from the ranks of an adventurous military aristocracy with strong ties of loyalty to its monarch. As was the case with Italy, France had also neglected to build up a reliable infantry of its own, but it compensated for this lack by employing Swiss and German foot soldiers. Despite their status as foreign mercenaries, these infantry companies proved to be valuable adjuncts to the native cavalry units. In addition, the French army enjoyed a clear superiority in artillery over all other European powers. In the end, however, the French forces were obliged to retreat back to their homeland less than a year after their initial incursion as a result of Ferdinand II of Aragon's decision to intervene to protect Spanish interests in the Kingdom of Naples. Even

Military Considerations

so, Charles VIII had clearly demonstrated the extent of Italy's vulnerability to foreign intervention and thereby initiated an intense rivalry among France, Spain, and Germany for control of its territories.

Machiavelli not only blames the plight of Italy in his own time on the degree to which rulers entrusted the defense of their states to mercenary soldiers but also argues, in chapter 13, that the same practice was the primary reason for the demise of Imperial Rome itself: "On considering the chief cause for the fall of the Roman Empire, we find it was solely that she took to hiring Gothic mercenaries. After that beginning, the Empire's forces steadily failed, for she stripped away all her own vigor to give it to the Goths" (1:54). In all likelihood, these lines contain an implicit criticism of his fellow Florentines, for he believed that the city's domination by financial and commercial interests had caused them to also lose their vigor and become effete. The same criticism could, of course, be directed at Milan and other major Italian cities that, like Florence, had lost their political independence despite the enormous wealth they possessed. It is perhaps inevitable that someone who had developed as a youth a consuming passion for Livy's history of the Roman people would feel alienated from a society of wool and silk merchants as an adult. A citizenry preoccupied with profits and losses, he believed, could never develop a fighting spirit or place the interests of the state over personal well-being. It is not that Machiavelli fails to appreciate the vital role that money plays in the prosecution of a war; he simply relegates it to a position of secondary importance. Nowhere does the Florentine secretary make this point more emphatically than in the *Discourses*, where in chapter 10 of book 2 he asserts: "I say, therefore, that not gold, as common opinion proclaims, but good soldiers are the sinews of war; for gold is not enough to find good soldiers, but good soldiers are quite enough to find gold" (1:350). As a case in point he notes that the valiant legionnaires of the Roman army never wanted for gold because it was brought to them even in their camps by those who feared them.

To reform a military system based on the use of mercenaries, Machiavelli advocates the creation of a civil militia composed of natives from the states—whether principalities or republics—that such a force would be charged with defending. A militia of this kind, he argues, should consist of infantry soldiers rather than the cavalrymen favored by the *condottieri*. In chapter 12 of *The Prince* Machiavelli takes the *condottieri* to task for this very bias by asserting: "This is the method they used: First, in order to give reputation to their own forces, they took away the reputation of the infantry.... And things came to such a state that in an army of twenty thousand soldiers there were not two thousand footmen" (1:51). The state's responsibility for training such citizen-soldiers is addressed in chapter 31 of book 3 of the *Discourses*. Here, Machiavelli declares that "an army evidently cannot be good if it is not trained, and it cannot be trained if it is not made up of your subjects. Because a country is not always at war and cannot be, she must therefore train her army in times of peace, and she cannot apply the training to others than subjects, on account of the expense" (1:500).

Machiavelli maintains that Cesare Borgia himself had been converted to the idea of a standing citizen militia. His conquest of Romagna, according to this argument, had proceeded in three stages. First, Cesare subdued the cities of Imola and Forlì with French auxiliaries that had been provided by Louis XII. Next, he employed mercenary armies led by such *condottieri* as Vitellozzo Vitelli and Oliverotto da Fermo to conquer other Romagnol cities like Pesara, Rimini, and Faenza. Lastly, when these *condottieri* proved faithless, he did away with them at Sinigallia and raised a citizen army of his own composed of men he conscripted in the duchy of Romagna. The last part of Machiavelli's analysis, however, is not in complete accord with the historical record. While it is true that Cesare did, in fact, raise a militia by conscripting one man per household during the crisis precipitated by the revolt of the *condottieri*, this force was assembled only as an emergency measure. Under Spanish commanders, it was used briefly at the recapture of Urbino and then quickly disbanded. The army that Cesare led back to Rome after the episode at Sinigallia, Machiavelli to the contrary notwithstanding, was composed strictly of mercenaries. The duke of Romagna clearly never outgrew the mentality of a *condottiere*.

It is known that Machiavelli himself had been pressing at least since 1503 for the formation of a civil militia that could be used to promote the political objectives of the Florentine republic. In that year, he asked

Military Considerations

Cardinal Francesco Soderini to assist him in persuading Piero Soderini, the prelate's elder brother and the gonfalonier of Florence, of the practicality of establishing a civil militia as a remedy for the republic's military deficiencies. Even with the cardinal's wholehearted support, it was not until December 1505 that the gonfalonier took it upon himself to obtain formal approval for the project from the Council of Eighty. From the very outset it was agreed that the recruits would be drawn exclusively from the rural districts of Tuscany since the cities under Florentine control were politically restive. For the next few months Machiavelli scoured the Tuscan countryside with the object of enrolling foot soldiers to serve under the flag of the republic. His efforts at recruitment soon bore fruit, and a formal parade by 400 members of the civil militia took place in the Piazza della Signoria on 15 February 1506 to the intense delight of the Florentine citizenry. One observer was so moved that he declared it to be the finest spectacle that had ever been organized in the city of Florence.

Machiavelli's aim was to establish a force numbering not less than 10,000 men who would be available at any time. These men could live in their own houses and pursue their normal vocations but would be required to report for duty whenever summoned. Their drills were modeled after those used by the Swiss (whose infantry Machiavelli greatly admired) and were generally confined to holidays. In addition, general musters of regional forces were held twice a year. Oddly enough, the man who became the commander of the militia was Michelotto da Corella, Cesare Borgia's sometime executioner and a cruel and much feared *condottiere* of Spanish origin. What particularly recommended him to Machiavelli, however, was the remarkable success of this professional soldier's efforts to impose military discipline on the Romagnol peasants who had been conscripted into Cesare's civil militia. He himself had seen these troops on parade at Imola during the fall of 1502 while he was there as an emissary on behalf of the republic. Machiavelli had little difficulty in convincing the gonfalonier that Don Michelotto was precisely the man who was needed to transform the raw recruits into soldiers. Even though many others had serious reservations about appointing a former henchman of Cesare Borgia's to such a sensitive post, Don Michelotto's commission as captain of the guard was duly ratified when it came up for a vote in the chambers of the Council of Eighty.

The fact that Don Michelotto enjoyed little support among the Florentine public actually turned out to be to his advantage, since the Council of Eighty was more inclined to ratify the appointment of someone who, in its opinion, would find it difficult to use the militia to promote his own political ambitions. For this very reason, they passed up the opportunity to bestow the commission on their fellow citizen Antonio Giacomini. Even this valiant soldier and ardent patriot, it was feared, might be tempted to use the new Florentine army to establish a tyranny of his own. Specific safeguards were subsequently established to ensure that anyone appointed to this post would pose no threat to the republic. In a decree passed on 6 December 1506, a committee known as the Nine of the Militia was created and charged with the responsibility of organizing the militia—including the election of a captain of the guard to be its commander. No native of Florentine territory, nor of any place within 40 miles of its borders, however, could be nominated to the post, according to a stipulation in the decree. Further stipulations prohibited each of the militia's eleven constables (battalion commanders) from being put in charge of companies recruited in his native district and from serving in any given command for more than one year. Such restrictions, it was believed, would prevent a constable from building up a loyal personal following among the men under his command. Shortly after their own selection, the members of the Nine of the Militia reconfirmed Don Michelotto in his position as captain of the guard and made Machiavelli, for all intents and purposes, the civil head of the militia by electing him chancellor-secretary of the committee.

The first extensive deployment of the militia against hostile forces occurred in the course of the campaign that Florence waged against the city of Pisa from the fall of 1508 to the summer of 1509. Strategically located at the mouth of the Arno River, Pisa had once been a thriving maritime republic that specialized in the silk and wool trade. To eliminate this threat to its own commercial supremacy and to gain direct access to the sea, Florence laid siege to the city in 1405 and after five months compelled it to surrender. The Pisans were never able to reconcile themselves

Military Considerations

to the harsh, punitive rule of their new masters and seized the opportunity to reclaim independence when the forces of Charles VIII occupied their city in the fall of 1494 en route to Florence. The loss of Pisa dealt a bitter blow to Florentine pride, but it was not until 15 years later that the political situation in the Italian peninsula permitted the republic to press its struggle with the Pisans to a decisive conclusion without fear of interference from a foreign or domestic power. Pisa was duly blockaded by sea and besieged by land. Machiavelli, as Soderini's personal representative, played a key role in coordinating the efforts of the Florentine land forces, two-thirds of which were units from the civil militia. Starved into submission, the Pisans gave up their 15-year struggle for independence and agreed to surrender unconditionally.

In recognition of the key role that the militia had played during the siege, Machiavelli was permitted to personally select a contingent of these troops and to march at its head when the Florentines made their formal entry into Pisa on 8 June 1509. Most citizens of Florence waxed ecstatic over their city's triumph, and many personal expressions of gratitude were subsequently sent to Machiavelli. One of his closest colleagues wrote him a letter hailing him as "a greater prophet than the Jews or any other generation ever possessed."[12] Totally overlooked in such tributes was the fact that Pisa had fallen by blockade and siege, not by assault. Hence, the militia had never really been tested by actual combat. A more rigorous test of its martial skill, however, was to occur a few years later when it had to face Spanish infantrymen of the Holy League.

The Holy League of 1511 was an alliance that Pope Julius II forged with Spain, Germany, England, and Venice in opposition to Louis XII of France. Soderini resisted all attempts to enlist Florence in the coalition, and after the French were forced to abandon almost all of their territorial holdings in Italy, Pope Julius permitted the restoration of Medicean rule in Florence as a means of punishing the republic for its failure to join the league. To press their claims, the Medici prevailed on Raimond da Cardona, the Spanish viceroy of Naples who had been placed in command of the league's army, to march on Florence with 5,000 of his foot soldiers during the late summer of 1512. These troops had seen extensive action in many of the battles that the league forces had fought in northern Italy earlier that year; by the time they reached Tuscan territory they were starving, unpaid, and without supplies of any kind. Soderini, full of confidence in the 10,000-man militia that Machiavelli had hastily assembled to meet the threat, unwisely turned down several opportunities to negotiate with Cardona. To stop Cardona, 4,000 of the militia were dispatched to garrison Prato—a heavily fortified city located 10 miles northwest of Florence. With only two outmoded artillery pieces at their disposal, the Spaniards had difficulty in breaching the city's walls, and their first attack was repulsed. In their second assault, however, a small breach in one of the walls was opened. Faced with the prospect of engaging in hand-to-hand combat with a determined foe, the men of the militia panicked and laid down their arms. For the next three weeks, Cardona's men killed, tortured, and ravaged without any moral restraint whatsoever. It is estimated that as many as 5,000 militia men and citizens of Prato fell victim to a "Spanish fury" similar to the wild orgy of theft, murder, and pillage subsequently perpetrated by the Spaniards at Antwerp in 1576. The terrifying sack of Prato completely destroyed the resolve of the Florentines to resist the restoration of Medicean rule, and Soderini was sent into exile at Siena on 1 September 1512 after 10 years of service in the post of gonfalonier for life. Approximately two months later, on 7 November, Machiavelli himself was "dismissed, deprived, and totally removed" from his official posts by a decision of the newly constituted *Signoria*. The Florentine militia was formally disbanded by the same body.

Despite the failure of the Florentine troops at Prato, Machiavelli's faith in the ultimate wisdom of entrusting the military fortunes of a republic or a principality to a civil militia never wavered. One of the key ideas propounded in *The Prince* is that victories won by mercenary troops are not really victories because once external enemies are disposed of, the *condottieri* themselves are apt to pose threats to the liberty of the states that rely on their services. Approximately two decades after the Prato incident, the Florentines themselves were to reestablish a civil militia as a response to a political crisis that grew out of the bitter conflict between Pope Clement VII and the German emperor Charles V. The dispute between the two sovereigns was quickly resolved in the

Military Considerations

emperor's favor. His forces captured Rome on 6 May 1527, and the pontiff was obliged to seek sanctuary in the prisonlike fortress of Castel Sant' Angelo. With Pope Clement thus isolated, the Florentines promptly expelled the entire Medici clan from the city and restored the republican form of government. In the meantime Pope Clement surrendered to Charles's troops; after being held prisoner for more than six months, he obtained his release by making many important concessions to the emperor. Sensing that a reconciliation between the two adversaries was in progress, the Florentines reestablished the militia during the summer of 1528.

The pope and the emperor did, in fact, sign a treaty, in June 1529. Clement agreed to invest Charles with the Kingdom of Naples and to crown him Holy Roman Emperor; Charles committed himself to reinstating Medicean rule in Florence. Some 40,000 German and Spanish troops were subsequently deployed against the republic in the fall of 1529. Opposing them was a civil militia of 13,000 men drawn from the rural districts of Tuscany and 3,000 men recruited from within the city itself, all of whom were placed under the command of a Florentine named Francesco Ferrucci. These forces were augmented by 5,000 mercenaries led by Malatesta Baglioni, a *condottiere* from Perugia. After his troops had made one futile attempt to escalade its walls, the commander of the imperial army decided to lay siege to Florence and starve its inhabitants into submission. Under the inspired leadership of Ferrucci, the civil militia performed heroically in keeping supply routes to the city open for almost an entire year. Ferrucci himself was eventually taken prisoner by imperial troops during a crucial engagement outside the walls and brutally executed a few hours later. With his death, the republic's prospects for survival were likewise dealt a fatal blow. Baglioni, for his part, repeatedly refused orders from the *Signoria* to attack the imperial army and even entered into independent negotiations with its commander. When the mercenary captain rejected the summons of the *Signoria* to surrender his commission, the gonfalonier ordered the militia to march against the traitor. Demoralized by the death of their commander and by the hopelessness of the military situation, the militia refused to comply with the gonfalonier's order. Seeing no other alternative, on 12 August 1530 the

Signoria signed a treaty that permitted the return of the Medici and thereby ended republican rule in Florence forever. Notwithstanding the republic's sudden demise, the militia's heroic deportment during the siege fully vindicated the faith in the military viability of such a force that Machiavelli had maintained from the early 1500s up until the time of his death in 1527.

In addition to the heroic efforts of the civil militia, it was also the walls of Florence that enabled it to withstand such a prolonged siege. Ironically, Machiavelli himself called Pope Clement's attention to the need for a thorough reappraisal of the city's fortifications in discussions he held with the pontiff at Rome during the spring of 1526. (The last such review had been conducted in 1494.) His proposal for the establishment of a five-member commission to oversee the reconstruction and fortification of the walls was approved in May 1526, and the new commission—called Curators of the Walls—duly elected Machiavelli as its secretary and quartermaster. From the very outset, a serious difference of opinion developed between the pontiff and the commission. Machiavelli and his colleagues recommended that a large area on the south bank of the Arno River be left outside the city's new defense perimeter since including it would prove too costly. Pope Clement, however, refused to countenance the exclusion of this area. To do so would have meant that the church of San Miniato al Monte might have to be abandoned to an enemy. San Miniato, it should be noted, is generally conceded to be the most beautiful Romanesque church in all of Florence. Moreover, it houses works by such Renaissance artists as Michelozzo Michelozzi, Lucia della Robbia, Antonio Pollaiuolo, and Antonio Rossellino. Owing to the impasse over the feasibility of fortifying this district, little significant work on the walls was actually completed by the commission during the year that Machiavelli served as its secretary.

Two years after the expulsion of the Medici in 1527, the question of the walls and their fortifications came to be a matter of crucial importance once again in view of the impending attack by the imperial forces. The *Signoria* of the reestablished republic decided to enlist the services of Michelangelo Buonarroti. Despite the fact that Pope Clem-

Military Considerations

ent had frequently commissioned him to execute many important architectural and artistic projects in the past, Michelangelo was most eager to assist the republic in its struggle to maintain its independence and prepared a number of designs for the defense of Florence, especially in the region of the hill of San Miniato where it was most exposed. To utilize his talents more fully, the *Signoria* elected him governor and procurator-general in charge of fortifications for all of Tuscany on 6 April 1529. In this capacity he was subsequently sent to Pisa, Livorno, and Ferrara to study their fortifications. He returned to Florence in September but, after only a few days, fled to Venice for reasons that are still unclear. Some allege that Michelangelo feared that Malatesta Baglione was about to betray the city to imperial forces. Others contend that his sudden flight was occasioned by his desire to put his money in a safe place for the sake of his family's financial security. In any event, the republic promptly declared him a rebel and outlawed him. Toward the middle of November Michelangelo was permitted to return to Florence after the authorities concluded that his services were indispensable to the city's defense. Once back, he duly resumed his position as governor of the fortifications. A month later he further demonstrated his loyalty to the republic by loaning the *Signoria* 1,000 ducats. When the city surrendered, Michelangelo sought refuge in the cloister of San Lorenzo. A short time later he was pardoned by Pope Clement, who was reported to have said, "Michelangelo is wrong, but don't do him any harm." Thereafter, he resumed work on statues for the sacristy and the library of San Lorenzo. At the end of 1533 Michelangelo received an invitation from the pontiff to create a mural depicting the Last Judgment for the altar wall of the Sistine Chapel, a work that he did not actually begin to paint until 1536 on commission from Pope Clement's successor, Paul III, and finally completed in 1546.

While various military problems pertaining to sieges are extensively analyzed in the seventh and final book of *The Art of War*, Machiavelli has next to nothing to say about the role of artillery in such operations. *The Prince* contains no references to artillery whatsoever. Machiavelli does not mention it even in chapter 20 when he discusses the utility of fortresses in the defense of a principality against foreign or domestic enemies. He simply argues, "A wise prince who is more afraid of his own people than of foreigners builds fortresses; he who is more afraid of foreigners than his own people rejects them. . . . Considering all these things, then, I praise one prince who builds fortresses and another who does not build them; I blame any prince who, trusting in them, considers the hatred of his people unimportant" (1:80–81). Implicit in Machiavelli's reasoning is the assumption that the disaffected citizenry of any given principality, unlike a foreign army, would have no access to artillery in attacking a fortress. It would, however, be a mistake to infer on this basis that he regarded artillery as a decisive factor in modern warfare. In fact, he argues quite to the contrary in the *Discourses*. In chapter 17 of book 2 he takes issue with those who hold that war will soon be reduced to the question of artillery. His general appraisal is that "artillery is useful in an army when the valor of the ancients is combined with it, but that without that, it is quite useless against a valorous army" (1:372). Some commentators find fault with Machiavelli for not having had the prescience to realize the tactical importance of artillery. Others contend that his judgment was a reasonable one at the time when he was writing.

In discussing a ruler's personal duties in the state's military affairs in chapter 14 of *The Prince*, Machiavelli unequivocally declares that "a wise prince, then, has no other object and no other interest and takes as his profession nothing else than war and its laws and discipline. . . . The chief cause that makes you lose your princedom is neglect of this profession, and the cause that makes you gain it is expertness in this profession" (1:55). He then specifies the type of training that will enhance a prince's military prowess. Hunting, for example, will not only accustom his body to endure physical hardships, it will also enable him to appreciate how crucial it is for a commander to acquire expertise in the topography of a region in which a military campaign is to be conducted. To exercise the mind his primary recommendation is that a prince read the histories of all peoples and reflect on the actions of renowned warriors recorded therein. By so doing, Machiavelli believes, rulers will better understand how to gain victory and avoid defeat. He also recommends that a prince select a single heroic personage from the past to serve as a model for imitation. Machiavelli finds ample precedent for this practice among the ancients themselves; he argues that Alexander the Great imitated Achilles, Julius Caesar emulated Alexander, and Scipio Africanus the Elder took Cyrus the Great as his model. The four chief exemplars from antiquity mentioned in *The Prince* are Moses, Cyrus, Romulus, and Theseus, but all in all, approximately 50 heroic figures from antiquity are singled out for praise in *The Prince* and the *Discourses*. That a majority are ancient Romans would appear to confirm the view that Machiavelli believed that Rome possessed more *virtù* than any other state. Most of these Romans, furthermore, lived prior to the outbreak of the First Punic War in 264 B.C. Thereafter, according to Machiavelli, the Roman state became increasingly corrupt and its citizenry less imbued with *virtù*.

The concept of imitation (*imitazione*) is thus a central ideological tenet of *The Prince*. Its rationale is succinctly stated at the outset of chapter 6. Here Machiavelli writes: "Since men almost always walk in the paths beaten by others and carry on their affairs by imitating—even though it is not possible to keep wholly in the paths of others or to attain the ability of those who you imitate—a prudent man will always choose to take paths beaten by great men and to imitate those who have been especially admirable, in order that if his ability does not reach theirs, at least it may offer some suggestion of it" (1:24). The value of imitating persons from antiquity in such spheres as medicine, philosophy, and the fine arts was, of course, widely accepted throughout the epoch of the Renaissance. Machiavelli's originality lay in broadening the concept to include the political and military achievements of the ancients. He addresses the question of imitating the governmental institutions of republican Rome in the *Discourses* and holds up its military organization as a model for contemporary armies in *The Art of War*.

The basis of the Roman army was the legion, a group consisting of about 4,000 infantrymen organized in maneuverable units of about 100 men (centuries). These soldiers, as well as the centurions who commanded them, wore light armor, a helmet, and a shield for protection and carried a short sword, a lance, and a javelin as weapons. For Machiavelli, the Roman legion is an ideal combat force that should be imitated by all peoples. In addition to superior organization, Machiavelli attributes much of the unrivaled efficacy of the Roman army to its thorough training and iron discipline. Near the end of book 7 of *The Art of War,* the general importance of these two factors is underscored: "Nature brings forth few valiant men; effort and training make plenty of them. Discipline does more in war than enthusiasm" (2:718).

10

Human Nature and State Religion

Machiavelli's most radical departures from traditional political thought are found in those parts of *The Prince* where he sets forth a thoroughly negative assessment of human nature and delineates its consequences for those who wield power in a principality. In chapter 15 he fully acknowledges that his advice to princes has no precedent: "And because I know that many have written about this, I fear that, when I too write about it, I shall be thought conceited, since in discussing this material I depart very far from the methods of others. But since my purpose is to write something useful to him who comprehends it, I have decided that I must concern myself with the truth of the matter as facts show it rather than with any fanciful notion" (1:57). A realistic understanding of human nature must, accordingly, be the basis of all valid political discourse. It is, moreover, because human nature remains essentially the same in all ages that Machiavelli finds the study of history to be of pragmatic value and recommends it so highly to his contemporaries.

Perhaps Machiavelli's boldest statement on human nature is found in chapter 17: "We can say this about men in general: they are ungrateful, changeable simulators and dissimulators, runaways in danger, eager for gain; while you do well by them they are all yours; they offer you their blood, their property, their lives, their children . . . when the need is far off; but when it comes near you, they turn about" (1:62). These remarks are offered in the context of the question as to whether it is better for a prince to be loved than feared. Because it is difficult for a ruler to elicit these emotional responses from his subjects simultaneously, Machiavelli concludes that fear is preferable to love because men have fewer compunctions about injuring someone they love than someone they fear. In addition, a ruler does not have it within his power to make his subjects love him, but he does possess the means to make them fear him. Engendering fear, therefore, has the advantage of permitting a prince to function with much more autonomy than would be the case if he chose to depend on the affections of others. Machiavelli insists, however, that a ruler should stop short of actually making himself hated.

After resolving the question of fear versus love, Machiavelli turns his attention to the relative merits of cruelty and clemency. To demonstrate the advantages of cruelty, he uses the example of the great Carthaginian general Hannibal. It was Hannibal's siege and capture of Saguntum—a city in Spain now called Sagunto, which was then allied with Rome—in 219 B.C. that was the proximate cause of the Second Punic War. Intending to crush Rome before it could fully mobilize its military resources, Hannibal undertook a bold invasion of Italy that required him to move an army of 35,000–40,000 troops over the Alps in the early autumn of 218 B.C. Approximately 26,000 of these men survived the arduous passage to reach the Italian city of Turin. Before long many disaffected Gauls from northern Italy and southern France allied themselves with the invaders. For the next 16 years Hannibal's forces lived off the land while campaigning throughout the peninsula. Among the many victories that the Carthaginians and their Gallic allies won during this period was the one at Cannae, where in 216 B.C. the 48,000 infantry and 6,000 cavalry that the Romans fielded were cut to pieces by Hannibal's augmented force of 35,000 infantry and 10,000 cavalry. Machiavelli expresses his own unqualified admiration for Hannibal by observing: "Among the most striking of Hannibal's achievements is reckoned this: though he had a very large army, a mixture of countless sorts of men, led to service in foreign lands, no discord ever appeared in it, either among themselves or with their chief, whether in bad or good fortune. This could not have resulted from anything else than his well-known inhuman cruelty, which, together with his numberless abilities, made him always respected and terrible in the soldiers' eyes; without it, his other abilities would not have been enough to get him that result" (1:63). He also cites the career of Cesare Borgia as an instance of a reputation for cruelty proving useful to a prince.

To illustrate the perils of excessive clemency, Machiavelli points to the example of Publius Cornelius Scipio Africanus (called Scipio the Elder)—Hannibal's chief adversary during the Second Punic War. The first charge Machiavelli levels against Scipio, whom he concedes was one of the most extraordinary leaders in the annals of world history, is that his leniency as a commander was the ultimate cause of the revolt among the Roman troops in Spain during the year 206 B.C. In 210 B.C. Scipio had been appointed chief commander of the Roman troops engaged in military operations against the Carthaginians in Spain. The rebellion to which Machiavelli refers took place after Scipio had succeeded in bringing all of Spain under Roman control; a full account of the incident may be found in book 28 of Livy's history. Anyone who peruses Livy's version of the event, however, will have difficulty in accepting Machiavelli's indictment of Scipio on the basis of excessive clemency. As reported by Livy, it was only when Scipio fell ill with a grave malady which was rumored to be fatal that many high-ranking officers under his command decided to take advantage of the situation by plundering Spanish cities and extracting monetary tribute from them. Since the legionnaires of lower rank had not been paid for a long time, it was relatively easy to persuade them to join the rebellion. But as soon as it became known that Scipio had fully recovered, the mutiny collapsed. Whereas Scipio chose to spare the rank-and-file legionnaires who had participated in the revolt, he exacted harsh retribution from the ringleaders. They were bound naked to stakes in a public square and scourged, after which they were beheaded. The spectators were reportedly so paralyzed by fear that there was no protest against the severity of the punishment. The following year, Scipio was elected consul and made governor of Sicily.

Machiavelli also charges Scipio with excessive clemency for his failure to discipline a subordinate who bore responsibility for atrocities committed against the populace of Locri. The inhabitants of Locri were the descendants of Greek colonists who had settled in the "toe" of southern Italy around 700 B.C., and the city was an ally of Rome at the outset of the Second Punic War. Shortly after Hannibal's victory at Cannae, Locri rebelled against the Romans and cast its lot with the Carthaginians. Machiavelli offers readers of *The Prince* few details of the incident for which he upbraids Scipio, and it is necessary to turn to book 29 in Livy's history for enough information from which to form a judgment. Livy relates that Scipio crossed over from Sicily to southern Italy in 205 B.C. and initiated a campaign to expel the Carthaginians from Locri and reassert Roman control over the territory. By this time the Locrians had become disillusioned with their African overlords and were inclined to welcome the Romans back. Hannibal attempted to prevent the loss of Locri but was put to flight by the Roman forces. Once in charge of the city Scipio punished those who had prompted its surrender to the Carthaginians over a decade earlier and bestowed their property on those citizens who had demonstrated their loyalty to Rome. Having accomplished his mission, Scipio left a force to defend the city under the command of a lieutenant named Quintus Pleminius and returned to Sicily. He soon felt obliged to return to Locri, however, after receiving reports about the abominable behavior of Pleminius and his men toward the city's inhabitants. After holding a formal inquiry into the accusations against Pleminius, he completely exonerated his deputy commander from any wrongdoing and permitted him to remain in charge of the garrison. Pleminius continued to oppress the Locrians, so they finally sent emissaries to plead their case with authorities in Rome. Pleminius was subsequently arrested, taken to Rome in chains, and held in prison until his death in 195 B.C.

Scipio's reputation apparently suffered little damage from his mishandling of affairs in Locri, for he soon received senatorial authorization to carry the war against the Carthaginians to Africa. In 204 B.C. Scipio landed in Africa with perhaps as many as 35,000 men and scored so many military victories during the following year that Hannibal himself was summoned back from Italy to defend Carthage. The struggle climaxed at Zama, where in 202 B.C. Hannibal's army was virtually annihilated and

Human Nature and State Religion

Carthage was forced to sue for peace. Hannibal was allowed to become chief magistrate of the defeated city. Under his administration, Carthage recovered so rapidly that Rome felt threatened once again. Fearing for his personal safety, Hannibal fled into exile. He first sought refuge in Syria and later in Bithynia, where he committed suicide to avoid being captured by the Romans.

A more extensive comparison between Hannibal and Scipio appears in the *Discourses,* where the argument as expounded in *The Prince* about the adverse effects of clemency is virtually turned on its head. In chapter 21 of book 3 Machiavelli argues that it is a leader's ability rather than his method that determines the success of his undertakings. The nature of the change in Machiavelli's position is summed up in the title of the chapter: "Why Hannibal, Whose Procedure Was Unlike Scipio's, Produced in Italy Effects Similar to Those of Scipio in Spain." Expatiating on this proposition, he contends that "Scipio, entering Spain, with that kindness and compassion of his quickly made that province his friend and made himself worshiped and loved by the people. On the other hand, Hannibal, entering Italy, with methods just the opposite—that is, with cruelty, violence, plunder, and every sort of perfidy—produced the same effects as Scipio did in Spain, for to Hannibal all the cities of Italy went over, all peoples followed him" (1:477). To explain the success of both Hannibal and Scipio, despite the differences in their temperaments, Machiavelli asserts, "Men are so eager for changes that most of the time there is as much desire for change among those who are well off as among those who are badly off, because, as I have said—and it is true—men are bored in good times and complain in bad ones. This desire, then, causes gates to open to any man who makes himself a leader of a revolution in a province" (1:477). In view of mankind's proclivity for change, any commander who inspires either love or fear—the two primal emotions that motivate men—can achieve political and military success provided that he himself possesses extraordinary ability (*virtù*). It is, of course, far more prudent in Machiavelli's judgment for a leader to make himself feared rather than loved if he wishes to instill obedience in those subject to his authority. There are inherent difficulties in both courses, however, that can lead to a ruler's downfall: whoever is too eager to be loved becomes an object of contempt; conversely, whoever tries too hard to inspire fear engenders hatred. Notwithstanding these pitfalls, Machiavelli does not counsel rulers to steer a middle course between love and fear. He rejects the middle course simply because it is incompatible with human nature: men are innately inclined to act in excessive ways. He concludes, however, that the careers of both Hannibal and Scipio amply demonstrate how extraordinary ability can atone for any excessive desire, whether to be loved or to be feared.

Machiavelli never attempts to explain how individuals like Hannibal and Scipio, or even Cesare Borgia, had managed to acquire the degree of *virtù* that enabled them to wield power so effectively. But Machiavelli finds the circumstances that imbue an entire people with greater *virtù* far more explicable, and the topic is addressed on several occasions in the *Discourses*. In the early parts of book 1, for example, Machiavelli assesses the relative merits of work done either of necessity (*necessità*) or by choice (*elezione*) and unequivocally asserts that greater virtue exists where choice is less of a factor. In chapter 3 he writes that "men never do anything good except by necessity, but where there is plenty of choice and excessive freedom is possible, everything is at once filled with confusion and disorder" (1:200). Even though hunger and poverty can make men industrious, Machiavelli freely concedes that it would be utter folly if a ruler did not endeavor to increase the level of prosperity throughout his principality. To counteract the enervating effects of affluence, however, wise rulers will enact laws and establish institutions that impose discipline on the citizenry. Surprisingly, in the preface to book 2, he confesses to a belief that the amount of *virtù* in the world remains constant from one historical epoch to another. It simply flourishes in different regions. According to this scheme, the world's *virtù* first arose in Assyria, then prospered among the Medians and Persians, and finally came to flourish in Italy and Rome. (Oddly enough, Machiavelli makes no reference to Greece.) After the fall of the Roman empire, it was the Franks, Saracens, and Turks who most strikingly manifested the attributes of *virtù*. In his own time, Machiavelli finds all the peoples of Germany to be worthy exemplars of *virtù*. Most lacking in *virtù*, on the other hand, are his contemporaries in Italy.

Human Nature and State Religion

In addition to the dictates of necessity and the influence of good laws, religion plays a crucial role in determining the degree of *virtù* that nations attain. Machiavelli's own views on God were unorthodox insofar as they were predicated on the proposition that all religions are strictly of human origin, but it is essential to recognize that he was always firmly committed to a belief in a supreme being. The importance he attached to religion is most clearly demonstrated in those parts of the *Discourses* where he argues that the men who have played the chief part in founding a religion are even more praiseworthy than those who have founded republics and kingdoms. In chapter 11 of book 1, accordingly, Machiavelli declares that Rome was far more indebted to Numa than to Romulus. Although Romulus is credited with founding the city in 753 B.C. and for being its first lawgiver, the creation of all Roman religious institutions is traditionally attributed to the efforts of Numa. According to Roman legend, he succeeded Romulus as king at the age of 40 in 715 B.C. and reigned for more than four decades until his death in 673 B.C. Machiavelli explains the importance of Rome's second king by declaring that "the religion introduced by Numa was among the chief reasons for the prosperity of that city. Because religion caused good laws; good laws make good fortune; and from good fortune came the happy results of the city's endeavors. And as the observance of religious teaching brings about the greatness of states, so contempt for it brings about their ruin" (1:225). One of the outstanding features of Numa's reign, although Machiavelli neglects to mention it, is that it was a time of uninterrupted peace. The doors of the temple of Janus, open in times of war, were closed for 43 years while he served as Rome's ruler.

Despite the pacific character of Numa's reign, Machiavelli contends that it was the system of ritualized worship which he developed that laid the foundation for Rome's prowess as a military power. The degree to which Rome's secular fortunes were intertwined with its religion was underscored by Cicero when he asserted, in the ninth section of a speech entitled "Concerning the Response of the Haruspices" (*De haruspicum responso*) that he delivered before the Senate in 56 B.C., that "we have overcome all nations of the world because we have realized that the world is directed and governed by the gods." The haruspices were

Etruscan soothsayers who interpreted the will of the gods as conveyed by certain natural phenomena as well as by the state of the entrails of sacrificial animals. They were often summoned to Rome to explain extraordinary meteorological events. Cicero's speech pertained to an occasion when they were called on to explain a strange noise that was reported to have been heard in a district located close to Rome. The haruspices had pronounced that expiation must be offered to the gods for certain general acts of impiety by the Roman people, and Cicero specified those acts in his speech.

Similar to the haruspices were the augurs, whose special gifts of divination included interpreting omens derived from the direction of flight or the various cries of birds. The augurs occupied a much higher position than the haruspices in the religious hierarchy of Rome because they had been organized into a college by Numa himself. (The haruspices were established as a college much later under the empire.) Numa also set up the institution of high priests called pontifices. The chief of these priests, the pontifex maximus, was entrusted with the duty of overseeing public ceremonies and private sacrifices as well as interpreting the will of heaven. Numa always maintained that he was advised on matters of state and religion by the nymph Egeria, with whom he frequently met in a sacred grove outside of Rome.

In waging war, the armies of the Roman republic sought to ensure themselves of divine support by various sacerdotal rituals. The commanders, for instance, formally vowed to dedicate part of any booty that might be garnered to the temples of certain gods. The Romans, moreover, had a ceremony which a college of priests known as *fetiales* (speakers) performed at the borders of enemy territory to demonstrate that the war about to be initiated was being waged in the defense of the state or its allies and therefore had divine sanction. The conviction that the gods themselves approved of their military expeditions must have had a considerable effect in making the troops more zealous in combat and in aiding the maintenance of Roman rule after victory. It is precisely because of the crucial role that religious factors played in the success of Moses that Machiavelli expresses some reservations, in chapter 6 of *The Prince*, as to whether the biblical patriarch should be included in a discussion of men who had become princes through their own merit, not through fortune: "And though Moses should not be discussed, since he was a mere executor of things laid down for him by God, nevertheless he ought to be exalted, if only for the grace that made him worthy to speak with God" (1:25). Clearly, Machiavelli recognizes that the conventions of religion are as useful as the example of exceptional individuals in promoting the objectives of civic greatness. While he himself was in charge of organizing the Florentine militia that was to be deployed against Pisa, public masses were celebrated in conjunction with the military drills that took place at formal assemblies. These public masses, it should be noted, were followed by exhortations pertaining to love of country and liberty.

To put Machiavelli's attitude toward the Church of Rome into proper perspective, it is necessary to recognize that he held two main grievances against the papacy—both of which are clearly spelled out in chapter 12 of book 1 of the *Discourses*. The first was that because of the bad moral example set by the papacy and its attendant ecclesiastical court, the Italians had become irreligious and perverse. The second was even more egregious in Machiavelli's eyes because it concerned Italian national unity. The Church had neither been able to occupy the whole of Italy nor had allowed anyone else to occupy it. Unity is essential, he maintains, because a populace is not happy unless all those who share an ethnic identity are brought under the jurisdiction of one republic or one prince, such as happened in France or Spain. In chapter 2 of book 2, moreover, Machiavelli broadens the scope of his critique of religion by challenging the ethical basis of Christianity itself. In the course of a comparison between the ancient pagans and the men of his own time, he writes:

> Pondering, then, why it can be that in those ancient times people were greater lovers of freedom than in these, I conclude it came from the same cause that makes men now less hardy. That I believe is the difference between our religion and the ancient.... This we infer from many of their institutions, beginning with the magnificence of their sacrifices, compared with the mildness of ours. There is in ours

some pomp, more delicate than magnificent, but no action either fierce or vigorous. In theirs neither pomp nor magnificence was lacking in the ceremonies, and in addition there was the deed of sacrifice, full of blood and ferocity in the slaughter of a multitude of animals; this terrible sight made men resemble it. Ancient religion, besides this, attributed blessedness only to men abounding in worldly glory, such as generals of armies and princes of states. Our religion has glorified humble and contemplative men rather than active ones. It has, then, set up as the greatest good humility, abjectness and contempt for human things; the other put it in grandeur of mind, in strength of body, and in all other things apt to make men exceedingly vigorous. (1:330–31)

Accordingly, the wicked are now able to prey upon the world because men, having paradise as their goal, are more inclined to consider how best to bear injuries rather than how to avenge them. As a partial remedy for the contemporary state of affairs, Machiavelli recommends that those responsible for interpreting religious scripture pay more attention to the importance of *virtù* and to the need to inculcate patriotic values in their adherents.

In chapter 18 of *The Prince* Machiavelli asserts that a ruler should strive to create the impression among his subjects that he is a man who is "all mercy, all faith, all integrity, all humanity, all religion." He then emphasizes the special importance of religion by observing: "No quality does a prince more need to possess—in appearance—than this last one. . . . Everybody sees what you appear to be; few perceive what you are, and those few dare not contradict the belief of the many, who have the majesty of the government to support them" (1:66–67). The essential point here is that princes, especially new ones, are frequently compelled to act contrary to the tenets of religion in order to keep their positions, and that if they succeed, their means will always be judged to have been honorable and will be everywhere praised. Friedrich Nietzsche expressly concurs with Machiavelli's amoral approach to politics in his posthumously published treatise entitled *The Will to Power* (*Der Wille zur Macht*). In section 925, written sometime during the summer or fall of 1888, Nietzsche asserts: "'Do not unto others that

Human Nature and State Religion

which you would not have them do unto you.' That counts as wisdom; that counts as prudence; that counts as the basis of morality—as the 'golden rule.' . . . But what if someone holding the *Principe* in his hands came forth and said: 'It is precisely such actions that one must perform, to prevent others from performing them first—to deprive others of the opportunity to perform them on us'?" (my translation).

11

The Pattern of History

To understand why an ardent republican like Machiavelli could write a treatise advising a prince on how to gain and maintain power, it is necessary to bear in mind that he was firmly convinced that some political objectives are best attained through the agency of a single individual rather than by any form of collective action. Machiavelli underscores this point in chapter 9 of book 1 of the *Discourses:* "This we must take as a general rule: seldom or never is any republic or kingdom organized well from the beginning, or totally made over, without respect for its old laws, except when organized by one man. . . . Nor will a prudent intellect ever censure anyone for any unlawful action used in organizing a kingdom or setting up a republic" (1:218). Clearly, according to this proposition, nearly all states—whether principalities or republics—owe their existence to the actions of one man. It would be a mistake, however, to conclude that Machiavelli failed to appreciate the importance of the citizenry. In chapter 58 of book 1, he acknowledges that, "if princes are superior to the people in establishing laws, forming communities according to law, setting up statutes and new institutions, the people are so much superior in keeping up things already organized that without doubt they attain the same glory as those who organize them" (1:317).

How best to expel the foreign armies from its soil was the foremost

The Pattern of History

political task confronting Italy during Machiavelli's lifetime, and he devotes the twenty-sixth and final chapter of *The Prince* to an impassioned exhortation calling for the liberation of his homeland from the "barbarians." The time is ripe, Machiavelli argues, for a new prince to unite Italy under his banner and to redeem it from all the ills brought about by the foreign intruders. Much of his exhortation was an attempt to persuade Lorenzo de' Medici, the duke of Urbino and sole nephew of Lorenzo the Magnificent, that the Medici family was divinely ordained to unite Italy and bring general happiness to its people. Even in summoning Duke Lorenzo to fulfill the historic mission of redeeming Italy, Machiavelli cannot resist alluding to Cesare Borgia:

> And though up to now various gleams have appeared in some Italians from which we might judge them ordained by God for her redemption, nevertheless we have seen later that, in the highest course of their actions, they have been disappointed by Fortune. Hence, as though without life, she awaits whoever he may be who can heal her wounds ... and cure her of those sores already long since festered. She is now praying God to send someone to redeem her from such barbarous cruelty and arrogance; she is now ready and willing to follow a banner, if only there be one who will raise it. (1:93)

Had Machiavelli succeeded in attaining his goal of becoming a mentor to Duke Lorenzo, he certainly would have paid scant heed to traditional morality in dispensing advice about the unification of Italy. The following general proposition, for example, is found in chapter 41 of book 3 of the *Discourses:* "This idea deserves to be noted and acted upon by any citizen who has occasion to advise his country, because when it is absolutely a question of the safety of one's own country, there must be no consideration of just or unjust, of merciful or cruel, of praiseworthy or disgraceful; instead, setting aside every scruple, one must follow to the utmost any plan that will save her life and keep her liberty" (1:519).

Machiavelli concludes the exhortation, and *The Prince*, with a stirring peroration in which he personally summons Duke Lorenzo to take up the task of unifying Italy.

Let your glorious family, then, undertake this charge with that spirit and that hope with which men undertake just labors, in order that beneath her ensign this native land of ours may be ennobled and, with her guidance, we may realize the truth of Petrarch's words:
> Valor against wild rage
> Will take up arms, and the combat will be short,
> Because ancestral courage
> In our Italian hearts is not yet dead. (1:96)

The quotation is from Francesco Petrarch's poem "My Italy" (*Italia mia*), which was composed at Parma in 1345 when the city was under siege by forces of the rulers of Mantua and Milan in an attempt to install an overlord to their own liking. "My Italy," formally addressed to the leaders of Italy, was an impassioned plea for the cessation of the pernicious internecine warfare that had made foreign intervention in peninsular affairs so tempting.

Although of Florentine stock, Petrarch was born in Arezzo in 1304 because his father had been exiled from Florence for political reasons two years earlier. In 1312, moreover, the family moved to Avignon in France, where the newly established papal court provided Petrarch's father with the opportunity to resume his former vocation as a notary. After studying law at Montpellier and Bologna, Petrarch took up the profession of man of letters and soon achieved such fame that kings, princes, and popes vied for the honor of playing host to his illustrious person. He made his first visit to Rome in 1337, and this experience made him realize just how much he loved Italy. Perhaps the high point of Petrarch's career came in April 1341, when he was crowned poet laureate at Rome in a ceremony held on the Capitoline Hill. Sometimes referred to as the father of the Italian Renaissance because of his pivotal role in initiating the humanist revival of learning, Petrarch yearned for a unified Italy under the leadership of a revived Rome. When he composed "My Italy," the unification of Italy seemed unlikely owing to the absence of a potential redeemer. A few years later, however, Petrarch became an ardent supporter of a visionary leader named Cola di Rienzi who took control of Rome and conferred the title of tribune upon himself. His political program was to restore the glories of the Roman state by creating a confederation of the free cities of Italy under the authority of an

The Pattern of History

emperor to be elected in Rome. He held on to power from 20 May to 15 December 1347, and again from 1 August to 8 October 1354, when he was hacked to death by a Roman mob that had found his rule oppressive and revolted against him. The historical counterpart of Rienzi in Machiavelli's lifetime was, of course, Cesare Borgia, whose political ambitions likewise came to an untimely end.

The aspirations held by Petrarch and Machiavelli for the unification and liberation of their homeland were, of course, entirely legitimate. But there is ample reason to question whether Machiavelli's vision of Italian grandeur was limited to the territory of Italy proper. According to Conor Cruise O'Brien, the concept of empire was never far from Machiavelli's political agenda. In *The Suspecting Glance* O'Brien invites the reader to reassess *The Prince* in light of the views the Florentine secretary expresses in "Tercets on Ambition." This long poem deals with the twin Furies of Ambition and Avarice, both of which he depicts as innate aspects of the human spirit that can never be completely exorcised. The best way to mitigate the adverse effects of Ambition in domestic realms is to direct its energy outward. "When through her own nature a country lives unbridled, and then, by accident, is organized and established under good laws, Ambition uses against foreign peoples that violence which neither law nor the king permits her to use at home (wherefore home-born trouble almost always ceases); yet she is sure to keep disturbing the sheepfolds of others, wherever that violence of hers has planted her banner." Machiavelli also addresses the problem of Italy's lack of martial vigor: "And when someone blames Nature if in Italy, so much afflicted and worn, men are not born so vigorous and hardy, I say that this does not excuse and justify our lack of worth, for discipline can make up where Nature is lacking. This in times gone by made Italy flourish, and for conquering the world from end to end, stern discipline gave her daring" (2:737). To give Machiavelli his full due, it should be pointed out that most of the poem focuses on the sufferings of innocent people who are subjected by conquerors to the violence of war. Although the date of its composition is not known with absolute certainty, it is generally believed that the poem was written near the end of 1509 and that it reflects Machiavelli's experience as a Florentine emissary at Verona when its inhabitants, both inside and outside the walls, were being robbed and pillaged by the forces of the German emperor Maximilian I. Others, including O'Brien, hold that the poem dates from 1516, thus making it fairly contemporaneous with the *Discourses*.

Oddly enough, even though the topic of expansion is specifically addressed in many sections of the *Discourses*, O'Brien makes no attempt to corroborate his thesis by citing any of the relevant passages from this treatise. In chapter 7 of book 1, for example, Machiavelli underscores the constancy of historical flux by asserting that "since all human affairs are in motion and cannot remain fixed, they must needs rise up or sink down; to many things to which reason does not bring you, you are brought by necessity" (1:210). A state might have a choice as to whether to expand or not, he concedes in chapter 1 of book 1, "if men were content to live on their own resources and were not inclined to govern others" (1:194). Since humans are a perverse lot, however, "it is impossible," he argues in chapter 19 of book 2, "for a republic to succeed in standing still and enjoying its liberties in its narrow confines, because if she does not molest some other, she will be molested, and from being molested rises the wish and the necessity for expansion" (1:379). This observation about republics is, of course, equally applicable to principalities. The underlying message is that if the citizenry of any state wishes to be secure in its own liberty at home, it must seek to expand abroad. Machiavelli analyzes the methods of expansion employed by the Tuscans, Romans, Spartans, and Athenians and concludes that the proper method was the one the Romans had adopted: namely, the formation of alliances in which Rome reserved for itself the headship—the seat in which central authority resided—and the right of initiative. Of course, the augmentation of Roman authority was at first achieved through the force of arms, but subjugated peoples were transformed into allies over time through a benign policy that granted them easy access to the honors and prerogatives of Roman citizenship.

Machiavelli did not, however, believe that a principality or republic could expand indefinitely, for he subscribed to the cyclical view of history set forth in the writings of the Greek author Polybius, who lived during the second century B.C. Polybius's life span coincided with the

The Pattern of History

period when Rome was consolidating its rule throughout the entire Mediterranean littoral. He himself was taken to Rome in 168 B.C. as a hostage along with no less than 1,000 other Achaeans for alleged opposition to Roman sovereignty. Once in Rome, Polybius led a very privileged existence as a tutor to Fabius and Scipio Aemilianus, the two sons of Aemilius Paulus. He soon became a close friend and adviser to Scipio, who eventually secured permission for Polybius and other surviving Achaean hostages to return to Greece 17 years later. After a short stay at home, he accompanied Scipio on several military campaigns, including the Third Punic War in which Carthage was finally destroyed in 146 B.C. After a similar fate befell Corinth in the same year, Polybius returned home and made good use of his high standing with the Romans to win whatever concessions he could on behalf of his defeated countrymen. He also continued to travel extensively, largely for the purpose of authenticating material to be incorporated into his chronological survey of the rise of Rome to the status of a world power—a process that Polybius viewed as the handiwork of providence. Polybius's *Histories,* as the work is called, originally consisted of 40 books and covered the period from the beginning of the First Punic War in 264 B.C. to the end of the Third Punic War in 146 B.C. Only the first five books are preserved in their entirety, but numerous fragments of varying length and epitomes from the others still exist. Polybius lived some 20 years after completing work on the *Histories* and met his death at the age of 82 after falling from a horse.

For anyone interested in ascertaining the extent of Polybius's influence on Machiavelli's historical and political theories, the most important parts of the *Histories* are the extant fragments from book 6. Here Polybius sets forth a cyclical theory of history in connection with his analysis of the three basic types of constitutional government: monarchy, aristocracy, and democracy. While all of these forms of government have certain advantages, each has an inherent tendency to fall into its own form of corruption that leads to instability. Thus, monarchy tends to degenerate into tyranny, aristocracy into oligarchy, and democracy into mob rule. When monarchy becomes tyranny, it is supplanted by aristocracy; and when aristocracy degenerates into oligarchy, it is abolished in favor of democracy. Finally, mob rule displaces democracy, and the cycle is completed. Polybius believes that two states—Sparta and Rome—were able to retard the cyclical course of history by adopting a "mixed" constitution that combined many of the qualities of monarchy, aristocracy, and democracy. He argues that Rome's constitution achieved a balance because of the way in which power was distributed between the monarchic consulship, the aristocratic Senate, and the democratic assembly of the people. Nonetheless, all states—including the Roman republic—are subject to decay and change for both external and internal reasons. Polybius lays down no fixed rules on the external agencies that affect decay because they are essentially unpredictable, but he finds that decay from within is a regular process. Once a state attains to supremacy, it is inevitable that a period of protracted prosperity will lead to a decline of civic virtue as its citizenry becomes more and more preoccupied with the acquisition of material goods and the pursuit of political prestige. Envy and resentment increase to the point where the citizens will no longer consent to obey but will claim all the prerogatives of the ruling class. In this fashion, democracy degenerates into mob rule, and this in turn sets the stage for a return to monarchy. Modern historians, it should be noted, fault Polybius for failing to recognize that the Roman republic was always dominated by an oligarchy despite the "mixed" character of its constitution. Both Livy and Machiavelli, however, fully accepted Polybius's idealized views on the political institutions of the Roman republic.

Also included in book 6 of Polybius's *Histories* is an extensive analysis of the Roman military system as well as a brief commentary on the civic value of the republic's religious traditions. Unquestionably, the fragments of book 6 exerted a profound influence on the development of Machiavelli's political philosophy. Still unresolved, however, is the question of how Machiavelli, who knew little Greek, came to be familiar with any of the contents of book 6. The first five books of the *Histories* had been translated into Latin by a humanist from Fano named Niccolò Perotti, who was commissioned to do so by Pope Nicholas V. These books were printed in 1473 and subsequently reissued several times before the end of the century. Interestingly enough, Perotti's translation concludes with a brief announcement about the fragment from book 6 that deals with the nature of the Roman constitution. Since Greek manu-

The Pattern of History

scripts of Polybius's *Histories* were readily available in several Florentine libraries, the content of the sixth book was undoubtedly familiar to many of Machiavelli's friends who gathered in the Ruccellai Gardens to discuss the Greek and Latin classics. These gardens were part of the palazzo, begun in 1446, that Leon Battista Alberti designed on commission for Bernardo Rucellai, the noted humanist who founded the Florentine academy known as the Orti Oricellari and later opened the Rucellai Gardens as a site for its meetings. Bernardo died in 1514, but his eldest son and heir, Cosimo, continued the practice of holding scholarly gatherings in the palazzo's gardens. Machiavelli became a habitué of these meetings at some indeterminate time after 1515, possibly as late as the middle of 1517, and read many parts of the *Discourses* to his learned friends (most of whom, ironically, were staunch partisans of the Medici) to obtain a critical appraisal of his arguments in favor of republican government. Machiavelli must have found these meetings highly stimulating since he decided to dedicate the *Discourses* to two members of the circle: Zanobi Buondelmonti, an aristocratic opponent of the Medici, and Cosimo Rucellai, a grandson of Bernardo.

Despite the absence of a single reference to Polybius in the *Discourses,* the influence of his doctrines is very much in evidence throughout the entire work. This is especially true of the second chapter in book 1, where Machiavelli virtually paraphrases many parts of the extant fragments from the sixth book of the *Histories*. For this reason, many critics now believe that the whole of the *Discourses* was written after 1515 and discount the idea that Machiavelli broke off its composition in 1513 to write *The Prince*. Those who still adhere to the older view that composition of parts of the *Discourses* actually precedes the composition of *The Prince* argue that Machiavelli may have learned what he needed to know about the sixth book of the *Histories* from Janus Lascaris, a Byzantine scholar who taught Greek in Florence and Rome for a number of years.

Chapter 2 in book 1 of the *Discourses* bears the title "How Many Kinds of Republics There Are, and the Kind of the Roman Republic." Machiavelli begins by taking issue with those writers who contend that there are but three kinds of government: namely, princedom, aristocracy, and popular government. In what appears to be an oblique reference to Polybius, he argues for an expanded typology:

> Some other and, as many think, wiser men hold that there are six kinds of government, of which three are very bad; the three others are good in themselves, but so easily corrupted that even they come to be pernicious. Those that are good are the three indicated above; those that are bad are three others, which evolve from these three, and each of these is in such a way like the one to which it is nearest that they all easily jump from one form to the other, for the princedom easily becomes tyrannical; the aristocracy with ease becomes a government by a few; the popular form without difficulty changes itself into one that abuses liberty. Hence if the founder of a state organizes one of these three governments in a city, he organizes it there for a short time only, because no precaution can be used to make certain that it will not slip into its contrary, on account of the likeness, in this case, of the virtue and the vice. (1:196–97)

Machiavelli deals with each of these transitions in detail before turning his attention to the merits of the Roman constitution. Here, too, he follows Polybius and extols the manner in which it achieved a balance between the monarchical, aristocratic, and democratic factions within the republic. Although such an arrangement greatly enhances the stability of the state, it cannot, however, render it permanently immune to the cyclical character of history. In chapter 6 of book 1, for instance, Machiavelli identifies expansion as one of the factors that leads to the weakening of a state and surveys the political fortunes of both Sparta and Venice in corroborating this proposition.

Unlike Rome, Sparta and Venice pursued inept policies in the course of their territorial expansion, and their newly acquired subjects revolted at the first opportunity. It would have been more prudent, Machiavelli contends, for such republics to have never attempted to increase their physical domains and to have restricted their military endeavors to building up impregnable defenses. In that way, they would have posed no threat to anyone because of their size, and potential enemies would have hesitated to assault them in view of their strong defenses. Nonetheless,

The Pattern of History

whether Sparta or Venice chose defense or expansion was irrelevant in the final analysis, for "if Heaven is so kind to her [a republic] that she does not have to make war, the effect might be that ease would make her effeminate or divided; these two things together, or either one alone, would cause her ruin" (1:210–11). There are six other passing references to the concept of ease (*ozio*), frequently translated as "idleness," within the *Discourses*. In chapter 55 of book 1, for example, he condemns the gentry (*ottimati*), "who without working live in luxury on the returns from their landed possessions, without paying any attention either to agriculture or to any other occupation necessary for making a living." Such men, he continues, are a plague in any republic and in every country "because men of these types are altogether hostile to all free government" (1:308–9). Again, in chapter 25 of book 2, he writes, "The disunion of republics usually results from idleness and peace; the cause of union is fear and war" (1:399).

Machiavelli's other two major statements on the cyclical view of history are to be found in chapter 5 of *The Golden Ass* (*Asino d'oro*) and in chapter 1 of book 5 of *The Florentine History*. Both of these statements make it clear that he believed the time was at hand for a rebirth of civic and military *virtù* among the Italians. *The Golden Ass* is an unfinished poetic epic in terza rima that was begun sometime during 1517. Its main plot was inspired by Apuleius's *Metamorphosis, or, The Golden Ass,* a novel in which the protagonist is magically transformed into an ass that, although speechless, still possesses human understanding. The narrator of Machiavelli's poem relates that, after becoming lost in a dark wood, he encounters a woman of uncommon beauty who takes him to her abode. Once there, he discovers that she is in the service of Circe and that he will shortly be transformed into an animal by the goddess herself in accordance with the magical powers that Homer describes in book 10 of the *Odyssey*. In Machiavelli's version of the manner in which this sorcery is carried out, the animal Circe transforms a human being into corresponds to his spiritual nature. The poem breaks off after the eighth chapter at a point when the narrator still does not know which animal Circe will find most appropriate for his forthcoming transformation. In an earlier episode, the narrator is left to spend a night by himself and makes use of this occasion to meditate on the cause of variations in earthly things. In reference to the cyclical nature of history and the fall of empires, he declares: "Ability makes countries tranquil, and from Tranquillity, Laziness next emerges, and Laziness burns towns and villages. Then, after a country has for a time been subject to lawlessness, Ability often returns to live there once again." This mutable state of affairs is then ascribed to the workings of the goddess Fortuna: "Such a course she who governs us permits and requires, so that nothing beneath the sun ever will or can be firm. And it is and always has been and always will be, that evil follows after good, and good after evil" (2:763). The narrator ends his meditation on a note of caution by reminding his readers that prayers and devotional ceremonies, though useful in strengthening morale, are no substitute for political and military activism in determining the course of events.

Many of the same points are likewise underscored in *The Florentine History*. Here, for example, Machiavelli argues:

> In their normal variations, countries generally go from order to disorder and then from disorder move back to order, because— since Nature does not allow worldly things to remain fixed—when they come to their utmost perfection and have no further possibility of rising, they must go down. Likewise, when they have gone down and through their defects have reached the lowest depths, they necessarily rise, since they cannot go lower. So always from good they go down to bad, and from bad rise up to good. Because ability brings forth quiet; quiet, laziness; laziness, disorder; disorder, ruin; and likewise from ruin comes order, ability; from the last, glory and good fortune. (3:1232)

The primary cause of Italy's degeneration, Machiavelli asserts, lay in its loss of military *virtù* during the greater part of the fifteenth century. Prior to the French invasion of 1494, military combat throughout the peninsula hardly deserved to be called "warfare." Men were not killed, cities were not sacked, and princedoms were not destroyed. It was, accordingly, the cowardice of those wars that opened the road to the barbarians and reduced Italy to a condition of slavery.

Machiavelli's view of Italy's plight in *The Florentine History* is, therefore, essentially the same as it was when he wrote *The Prince* nearly

The Pattern of History

a decade earlier. Even though there is no evidence that Machiavelli had already adopted the cyclical theory of history as far back as 1513, his belief in the imminence of Italy's redemption was just as strong then as it was after he became familiar with the sixth book of Polybius's *Histories*. Ample testimony to this effect may be found in the final chapter of *The Prince*: "Having taken account, then, of everything discussed above [that is, throughout the preceding 25 chapters of *The Prince*], and meditating whether at present in Italy conditions so unite as to offer a new prince glory, and whether the matter to be found here assures to a prudent and able ruler a chance to introduce a form that will bring him glory and her people general happiness, I believe so many things now join together for the advantage of a new prince that I do not know what time could ever be more fit for such a prince to act" (1:92–93).

12

Posthumous Notoriety of *The Prince*

It was not until the Roman Catholic Church responded to the challenge posed by the Protestant Reformation by initiating its own Counter Reformation during the 1550s that the morality of *The Prince* and the character of Machiavelli came into disrepute. In 1559, despite the fact that the treatise had borne the imprimatur of Pope Clement VII when it was originally published in 1532, it was placed on the Index of Prohibited Books (*Index librorum prohibitorum*) along with Machiavelli's entire oeuvre. The Index was created by Pope Paul IV in 1557 and effectively banned open dissemination of any book that was deemed morally reprehensible by the Church. It was actually at the behest of the Society of Jesus that Pope Paul issued the decree that placed Machiavelli's writings on the Index, a decision that was formally confirmed five years later in 1564 by the churchmen attending the Council of Trent. Not content with an official proscription of his writings, several Spanish and Italian members of the Jesuit order over the next century published treatises devoted to exposing the evils of "Machiavellianism." The unremitting hostility of the Jesuits toward Machiavelli was apparently based on their image of him as a zealous advocate of the subordination of the Church to the state. The influence of the Jesuit order was to wax and wane over the

Posthumous Notoriety of The Prince

succeeding centuries, but Machiavelli's works would not be removed from the Index until 1890.

Machiavelli's doctrines were introduced to the French court through the auspices of Catherine de' Medici, Lorenzo the Magnificent's great-granddaughter who married the duke of Orléans who became Henry II of France in 1547. Three of her four sons successively became kings of France following the death of her husband in 1559: Francis II, Charles IX, and Henry III. It was during the reign of her son Charles IX that the horrific Saint Bartholomew's Day massacre occurred on 24 August 1572. On that day, some 3,000 French Protestants, commonly known as Huguenots, were slaughtered in Paris, and probably double that number perished in the rest of France. There is no question but that the queen-mother herself, along with some confederates from the Guise family, instigated the massacre for what she perceived to be a *raison d'etat*. A literary response to the event was penned by a Huguenot named Innocent Gentillet and published anonymously in 1576 under the title, *Discourse on the Manner of Governing and Maintaining a Kingdom or Other Principality in Proper Peace . . . Against Nicholas Machiavelli the Florentine (Discour sur les moyens de bien gouverner et maintenir en bonne paix un royaume ou autre principauté . . . contre Nicolas Machiavel Florentin)*. In it, Gentillet deplores the tyranny over the French nation by the devotees of Machiavelli's doctrines, Catherine de' Medici and her court of Italians and Italianized Frenchmen. Ironically, the work was dedicated to the youngest son of Catherine de' Medici, Duke François d'Alençon, who strongly opposed his mother's political policies. Charles IX died two years after the massacre of the Huguenots and was succeeded by his brother Henry III. When King Henry fell victim to an assassin in 1589, he is reported to have had a copy of *The Prince* on his person. Owing to the premature death of Duke François d'Alençon, the crown of France was passed on to a member of the Bourbon family who reigned as Henry IV until his own assassination in 1610. Like his predecessor, he too was said to be carrying a copy of *The Prince* when the assassin struck. Oddly enough, Henry IV was actually raised as a Huguenot and had been obliged to feign conversion to Catholicism to escape death during the massacre of 1572. A few years after his ascension to the

French throne, he abjured his Protestant faith a second time as part of a Machiavellian maneuver to secure the loyalty of his Catholic constituency and is alleged to have subsequently remarked, "Paris is well worth a Mass."

Even though an English translation of *The Prince* did not appear until 1640, it was the frequent allusions to Machiavelli in plays by Elizabethan dramatists such as Christopher Marlowe, William Shakespeare, and Ben Jonson that did most to popularize his image as an evil counselor. It is generally assumed that the Elizabethan public was somewhat familiar with *The Prince* from earlier French translations of the work. In Marlowe's *The Jew of Malta*, a melodrama probably written around 1589 but not printed until 1632, the plot focuses on the villainous career of a Maltese Jew named Barabas. This character is introduced by Machiavelli himself as one of his disciples in a lyrical 35-line prologue. Midway through the prologue, "Machiavel" asserts:

> Though some speak openly against my books,
> Yet will they read me, and thereby attain
> To Peter's chair; and when they cast me off,
> Are poisoned by my climbing followers. (pro. 10–13)

Shakespeare's references are far more casual. In *The Merry Wives of Windsor*, for example, the host of the Garter Inn asks the French physician Caius: "Am I politic? Am I subtle? Am I a Machiavel?" (3.1. 95–96). Likewise, in Part One of *Henry VI*, when York is informed by Joan La Pucelle that Alençon is the man responsible for her pregnancy, he responds with the words: "Alençon! that notorious Machiavel!" (5.4.4). In Part Three of this trilogy, York boasts that he can deceive more slyly than Ulysses was capable of doing "and set the murderous Machiavel to school" (3.2.193). In Jonson's *Volpone, or The Fox* the pompous English knight named Sir Politic Would-Be advises a countryman in the rules of travel. One of the precepts he recommends is to profess no religion whatsoever since the secular laws of any realm are all that truly matter. To bolster this argument, Sir Politic cites as his authorities both "Nick Machiavel and Monsieur Bodin" (4.1.26). Unlike Marlowe and

Posthumous Notoriety of The Prince

Shakespeare, however, Jonson had firsthand knowledge of the contents of *The Prince,* and this crude distortion of Machiavelli's doctrines, as well as those of Jean Bodin, is intended to expose Sir Politic's spurious claim to erudition.

Still, Jonson does fault Machiavelli for his lack of compassion. In *Timbers, or Discoveries Made upon Men and Matter,* a miscellaneous collection of notes, jottings, and miniature essays that was first published in 1640, he declares: "A *Prince* should exercise his cruelty, not by himselfe, but by his Ministers: so hee may save himselfe, and his dignity with his people, by sacrificing those, when he list, saith the great *Doctor* of *State, Macchiavell.* But I say, he puts off man, and goes into a beast, that is cruell." In opposition to Machiavelli, he argues the merits of clemency as the preeminent princely virtue. He also disapproves of Machiavelli's counsel to princes about halfhearted implementation of cruel measures: "*Hee* that is cruell to halfes, (saith the said *St. Nicolas*) looseth no lesse the opportunity of his cruelty, then of his benefits: For then to use his cruelty, is too late; and to use his favours will be interpreted feare and necessity; and so hee looseth the thankes. Still the counsell is cruelty."[13]

Most noteworthy among the tracts written by Germans in opposition to *The Prince* is the one composed by Frederick the Great of Prussia at the age of 27 while he was still a crown prince. The idea of writing a chapter-by-chapter refutation of *The Prince* grew out of the correspondence that he had been conducting with Voltaire since the summer of 1737 on various literary and political topics. In a letter dated 22 March 1739, after a prior exchange of views on Machiavelli's doctrines, he first announced his intention of writing a refutation of *The Prince*. The response of his mentor was most encouraging, and Frederick spent the fall and winter of 1739 working on the project. As he completed portions of his refutation, he sent them on to Voltaire for editorial revision. It was Voltaire who eventually affixed the title of *Antimachiavel* to the manuscript and arranged to have it published by a printer in The Hague. Frederick subjects *The Prince* to a critique that is rooted in the optimistic assumptions of the Enlightenment. Like many others who lived during that epoch, he vastly overestimated the power of reason to subdue the elemental passions of mankind. Accordingly, although

Frederick acknowledges that the conditions prevailing in Italy during the sixteenth century may have justified the commission of immoral acts by its rulers, he also contends that Machiavelli's tenets have lost much of their validity in view of the general advance in public morality since then. Most important, he rejects Machiavelli's negative appraisal of human nature.

Shortly after the publication of *Antimachiavel,* Frederick himself became king of Prussia upon the death of his father, Frederick William, on 31 May 1740. Concerned that some passages in the treatise might offend other rulers, he petitioned Voltaire to have it withdrawn from circulation; however, the attempt at suppression failed because of the printer's refusal to cooperate. Anyone familiar with Frederick's subsequent career as a monarch cannot fail to conclude that he proved to be one of the most faithful adherents of the Machiavellian principles that he so fiercely denounced in his own commentary on *The Prince*. Perhaps Voltaire anticipated Frederick's change of heart, for when the two met at a small castle near Cleves later in 1740, he is reported to have said: "Sir, had I been Machiavel, and been permitted to have access to a young King, my first advice to him would have been, to write against me."[14]

A lesser known instance of Machiavelli's influence, albeit a highly perverted one, is reflected in a tract known as *The Protocols of the Learned Elders of Zion*. This spurious document purports to be the record of a series of secret meetings that took place at Basel, Switzerland, during the first Zionist congress in the year 1897. At these meetings the Jews and the Freemasons reportedly laid out plans to undermine Christian civilization by promoting liberalism and socialism for the purpose of establishing a world state that would be under their joint control. When published in Russia during the early 1900s, the document was widely accepted as authentic. It was subsequently translated into other European languages and did much to foster anti-Semitic sentiment in both Europe and the United States. The first step in exposing the fraudulent character of the *Protocols* was taken in 1921: the British journalist Philip Graves demonstrated that much of the tract's content had been derived from a satire on the policies of Emperor Napoleon III by a French lawyer named Maurice Joly, a work that had been published in 1864 under the title, *Di-*

Posthumous Notoriety of The Prince

alogue in Hell between Machiavelli and Montesquieu, or, The Politics of Machiavelli in the Nineteenth Century by a Contemporary (Dialogue aux enfers entre Machiavel et Montesquieu, ou, la politique de Machiavel au XIXe siècle, par un contemporain). Joly, a republican opponent of the Second Empire, published this ironical manual of cheating and duplicity anonymously while in exile. Perhaps the inspiration for his satire came from an apocryphal story to the effect that shortly before his death Machiavelli had a dream of the Last Judgment in which he was allowed to choose whether he wished to go to heaven or to hell. After comparing the rabble who were on their way to heaven with the distinguished company of philosophers who were still debating political questions on their way to hell, he promptly asked to be consigned to the netherworld. In Joly's work, Machiavelli and Baron de Montesquieu step forth and expatiate on the ideological content of their respective masterworks—namely, *The Prince* and *The Spirit of Laws* (*De L'Esprit des lois*). The link between Napoleon III and Machiavelli, it should be noted, is far from arbitrary, for it was widely known that *The Prince* was the chief source of the French emperor's ideas on governance. In the main, the ideas attributed to Machiavelli by Joly are the ones that found their way into the *Protocols*. According to research by Soviet historians, the document is a forgery that was concocted by the Czarist secret police—an organization known as the Ochrana. In addition to Joly's work, the same researchers have identified several other sources that entered into the compilation of the *Protocols*.

A more legitimate, though hardly more complimentary appropriation of Machiavellian doctrine appears in the treatise *Studies in Machiavellianism* that Richard Christie and Florence L. Geis published in 1970. Produced under the auspices of Stanford's Center for Advanced Study in the Behavioral Sciences, this study in social psychology attempts to answer the question of whether someone who agrees with Machiavelli's ideas behaves differently from someone who disagrees with him. For Christie and Geis, the individual with a "Machiavellian" personality views others as objects to be manipulated for his own purpose. A successful manipulator of this type possesses the following characteristics: (1) a lack of empathy in interpersonal relationships, (2) a low regard for conventional morality, (3) a nonpathological perception of objective reality, and (4) an ability to sacrifice long-range ideological goals for the sake of achieving immediate tactical ends. To test for these attributes, *The Prince* and the *Discourses* were scanned for statements that could be used in the construction of a diagnostic system of measurement known as the Machiavellianism Scale or, for short, the Mach Scale. Machiavelli's language was, of course, suitably altered when necessary, and the material culled from the aforementioned works was supplemented by statements of similar import—such as, "Barnum had it right when he asserted that there's a sucker born every minute." Responses to each of these items were ranked on a one-to-seven scale: "strongly disagree, somewhat disagree, slightly disagree, neutral, slightly agree, somewhat agree, and strongly agree."[15] An elaborate series of experiments then determined the degree of correspondence between an individual's score on the Mach Scale and his actual behavior. It was found that Machiavellianism was generally higher for males as well as for people with an urban background. Even though there was no demonstrable connection between Machiavellianism and an ability to score higher on standardized tests of intelligence, occupational success in later life was ascertained to be correlated with one's ranking on the Mach Scale. Such a correlation was especially strong among women and among those with a college education. The general conclusion of the study is that modern society is becoming increasingly similar in structure to the laboratory situations in which those with Machiavellian attitudes win.

Christie and Geis's decision to name their test as they did is, of course, perfectly understandable in light of the long-established practice of using Machiavelli's name as an eponymn for duplicity and unscrupulous scheming in personal conduct or for the pursuit of statecraft at the expense of morality. The first recorded use of the term *Machiavellianism*, according to the *Oxford English Dictionary*, dates back to 1629. Its adjectival forms *Machiavel* and *Machiavellian* are even older. The *OED* cites a 1570 example: "proud contempnars or machiavel mokkaris of all religioun and vertew." Another from 1579 is the assertion, "thys absurd manner of reasoning is very mackiaullian logick." Christie acknowledges that his own interest in manipulative behavior

Posthumous Notoriety of The Prince

stemmed from an impression of Machiavelli to be found in John Webster's play *The White Devil* (1612), in which one of the characters asserts: "Those are found weighty strokes which come from th'hand, / But those are killing strokes which come from th'head. / O the rare tricks of a Machivillian!" (5.3.194–96).

In view of the extent to which Machiavellianism has become part of the popular imagination, it was inevitable that some inventive writer would take poetic license with the historical Machiavelli and turn him into a fictive figure who himself ends up the victim of others' deception. Such a role reversal is, in fact, the basis of W. Somerset Maugham's novel *Then and Now* (1946). For the most part, the action takes place during a three-month period starting in October 1502, when Machiavelli has joined Cesare Borgia in his reconquest of Romagna and culminates with the duke's triumph over the disloyal *condottieri* at Sinigallia. The plot unfolds on two interrelated levels: one part of the narrative charts Machiavelli's political education during Cesare's campaign, and the other part deals with Machiavelli's stratagems to seduce a married woman from Forlì with whom he has become infatuated. His attempt to seduce this woman comes to naught, but that of a nephew who serves as his page succeeds. At the end, Machiavelli is left to ponder his nephew's betrayal, as well as that of six or more other people who had participated in the deception. While Maugham's novel revolves entirely around the "then" in the title, the "now" of it implies that contemporary political and amorous intrigues are essentially what they were in sixteenth-century Italy, and always will be.

Notes

1. Quoted in Robert B. Downs, *Books that Changed the World* (New York: New American Library, 1956), 26.

2. Although written in 1534, this treatise was first published in 1857 when it was included in the 10-volume edition of Francesco Guicciardini, *Opera inedite* (Florence: Barbera, Bianchi, e Comp., 1857–1867).

3. *The Philosophical Works of Francis Bacon,* ed. John M. Robertson (Freeport, N.Y.: Books for Libraries Press, 1970), 141.

4. Ibid., 153; Bacon's italics.

5. Ibid., 164; Bacon's italics.

6. Thomas Babington Macauley, *Critical, Historical, and Miscellaneous Essays* (Boston: Houghton, Osgood, and Co., 1878), 1:267–68.

7. Ibid., 1:309.

8. Ibid., 1:311.

9. Jean-Jacques Rousseau, *On the Social Contract with Geneva Manuscript and Political Economy,* ed. Roger D. Masters, trans. Judith R. Masters (New York: St. Martin's Press, 1978), 88.

10. "The Modern Prince," in *Selections from the Prison Notebooks of Antonio Gramsci,* ed. and trans. Quintin Hoare and Geoffrey Nowell Smith (London: Lawrence and Wishart, 1971), 135.

11. Conor Cruise O'Brien, *The Suspecting Glance* (London: Faber and Faber, 1972), 15–31.

12. Letter dated 17 June 1508 from Filippo da Casavecchia to Machiavelli. Quoted in Pasquale Villari, *The Life and Times of Niccolò Machiavelli,* trans. Linda Villari (New York: Scribner's, 1891; reprint, New York: Haskell House, 1969), 1:460.

13. *Ben Jonson: The Poems/ The Prose Works,* ed. C. H. Herford, Percy Simpson, and Evelyn Simpson (London: Oxford University Press, 1954), 8:599-600.

14. Quoted in Theodore Besterman, *Voltaire* (Chicago: University of Chicago Press, 1969), 632.

15. Richard Christie and Florence L. Geis, *Studies in Machiavellianism* (New York: Academic Press, 1970), 28.

Selected Bibliography

Primary Works

Editions of Machiavelli's Works

The Chief Works and Others. 3 vols. Translated and edited by Allan Gilbert. Durham, N.C.: Duke University Press, 1965. Over 1,500 pages in length, this three-volume set is the most extensive collection of Machiavelli's writings currently available in English translation. Although textual annotations are minimal, there are succinct introductions to the individual selections and a comprehensive index to the entire corpus. The most convenient edition of Machiavelli's collected works in Italian is *Tutte le opere,* edited by Mario Martelli (Florence: Sansoni, 1971). Those interested in consulting an Italian text of *The Prince* equipped with an extensive critical apparatus in English (except for quotations from foreign-language sources) should refer to *Il principe,* edited by L. Arthur Burd (Oxford: Clarendon Press, 1891). Also noteworthy for those concerned with the Italian text is *Machiavelli's "The Prince": A Bilingual Edition,* translated, introduced, and edited by Mark Musa (New York: St. Martin's Press, 1964).

Outstanding Editions of *The Prince* in English

The Prince. Translated and introduced by George Bull. Harmondsworth, Eng.: Penguin Books, 1961.

"The Prince" *by Niccolò Machiavelli.* Translated, introduced, and edited by Daniel Donno. New York: Bantam Books, 1966.

The Prince. Translated, introduced, and edited by James B. Atkinson. Indianapolis: Bobbs-Merrill, 1976.

The Prince: A Norton Critical Edition. Translated and edited by Robert M. Adams. New York: W. W. Norton, 1977.

The Prince: A New Translation. Translated, introduced, and annotated by Harvey C. Mansfield, Jr. Chicago: University of Chicago Press, 1985.

Other Works in English Translation

"*The Art of War*" *of Niccolò Machiavelli.* Translated by Ellis Farneworth and revised with an introduction by Neal Wood. New York: DaCapo Press, 1990.

The Comedies of Machiavelli: The Woman from Andros, The Mandrake, Clizia: A Bilingual Edition. Translated and edited by David Slices and James B. Atkinson. Hanover, N.H.: University Press of New England in conjunction with Dartmouth College, 1985.

The Discourses. Edited and introduced by Bernard Crick; translated by Leslie J. Walker with revisions by Brian Richardson. Harmondsworth, Eng.: Penguin Books, 1970.

"*The Discourses*" *of Niccolò Machiavelli.* 2 vols. Translated, introduced, and annotated by Leslie J. Walker, with a new introduction and appendices by Cecil H. Clough. London: Routledge & Kegan Paul, 1975.

Florentine Histories. Translated by Laura F. Banfield and Harvey C. Mansfield, Jr., with an introduction by Harvey C. Mansfield, Jr. Princeton, N.J.: Princeton University Press, 1990.

The Letters of Machiavelli. Translated, introduced, and edited by Allan Gilbert. New York: Capricorn Books, 1961.

The Literary Works of Machiavelli: Mandragola, Clizia, A Dialogue on Language, and Belfagor. Translated and edited by John Rigby Hale. London: Oxford University Press, 1961.

The Portable Machiavelli. Translated, introduced, and edited by Peter Bondanella and Mark Musa. New York: Viking Press/Penguin Books, 1979.

Selected Bibliography

Secondary Works

Biography

De Grazia, Sebastian. *Machiavelli in Hell.* Princeton, N.J.: Princeton University Press, 1989.

Hale, John Rigby. *Machiavelli and Renaissance Italy.* New York: Macmillan, 1960.

Marcu, Valeriu. *Accent on Power: The Life and Times of Machiavelli.* Translated by Richard Winston. New York: Farrar & Rinehart, 1939.

Muir, D. Erskine. *Machiavelli and His Times.* London: Heinemann, 1936.

Ridolfi, Roberto. *The Life of Niccolò Machiavelli.* Translated by Cecil Grayson. Chicago: University of Chicago Press, 1963.

Roeder, Ralph. *The Man of the Renaissance. Four Lawgivers: Savonarola, Machiavelli, Castiglione, Aretino.* New York: Viking Press, 1933.

Villari, Pasquale. *The Life and Times of Niccolò Machiavelli.* 2 vols. Translated by Linda Villari. New York: Scribner's, 1891. Reprint. New York: Haskell House, 1969.

Critical Studies

Books

Anglo, Sydney. *Machiavelli: A Dissection.* New York: Harcourt, Brace & World, 1969. A comprehensive survey of Machiavelli's writings that restricts itself to an interpretation of primary sources.

Bondanella, Peter E. *Machiavelli and the Art of Renaissance History.* Detroit: Wayne State University Press, 1973. A chronological analysis of Machiavelli's development as a literary stylist that focuses on the compositional techniques employed in the depiction of heroic personages.

Burnham, James. *The Machiavellians: Defenders of Freedom.* New York: John Day, 1943. Reprint. Washington, D.C.: Regnery Gateway, 1987. A spirited defense of Machiavelli as a purveyor of political realism whose teachings are of immense value to those committed to the preservation of liberty.

Christie, Richard, and Florence L. Geis. *Studies in Machiavellianism.* New York: Academic Press, 1970. An attempt to probe the question of whether a person who agrees with Machiavelli's ideas behaves differently from one who disagrees with him.

Fleisher, Martin, ed. *Machiavelli and the Nature of Political Thought.* New York: Atheneum, 1972. A collection of papers presented at York University,

Toronto, during a conference commemorating the five-hundredth anniversary of Machiavelli's birth.

Gilbert, Allan H. *Machiavelli's "Prince" and Its Forerunners: "The Prince" as a Typical Book* de Regimine Principum. Durham, N.C.: Duke University Press, 1938. Reprint. New York: Barnes & Noble, 1968. An attempt to demonstrate how much *The Prince* has in common with other books of advice to princes that were familiar to Machiavelli and his contemporaries.

Hulliung, Mark. *Citizen Machiavelli.* Princeton, N.J.: Princeton University Press, 1983. An explication of Machiavelli's thought in terms of its subversion of traditional humanistic values.

Meinecke, Friedrich. *Machiavellism: The Doctrine of* Raison d'Etat *and Its Place in Modern History.* Translated by Douglas Scott. New Haven, Conn.: Yale University Press, 1957. A definitive examination of Machiavelli's role in the development of modern political theory.

Pitkin, Hanna Fenichel. *Fortune Is a Woman: Gender and Politics in the Thought of Niccolò Machiavelli.* Berkeley: University of California Press, 1984. A pioneering study of the role of gender in political theory that depicts Machiavelli, largely because of the way he personifies the concepts of *virtù* and *fortuna,* as a misogynistic authoritarian.

O'Brien, Conor Cruise. *The Suspecting Glance.* London: Faber and Faber, 1972. A provocative exposition of the darker side of Machiavelli's doctrines.

Pocock, John Greville Agard. *The Machiavellian Moment.* Princeton, N.J.: Princeton University Press, 1975. A major work whose principal aim is to underscore the influence of Machiavelli on English and American political thought of the seventeenth and eighteenth centuries.

Prezzolini, Giuseppe. *Machiavelli.* Translated by Gioconda Savini. New York: Farrar, Straus & Giroux, 1967. Best survey of the ways in which Machiavelli's doctrines have been interpreted by subsequent generations.

Raab, Felix. *The English Face of Machiavelli: A Changing Interpretation, 1500–1700.* London: Routledge & Kegan Paul, 1965. Charts the role played by Machiavelli in effecting the decline of religion as a factor in the development of modern political theory.

Ruffo-Fiore, Silvia. *Niccolò Machiavelli.* Twayne's World Authors Series. Boston: Twayne/G. K. Hall, 1982. An astute analysis in which the writings of Machiavelli are examined in terms of the interaction of politics, history, and literature.

Skinner, Quentin. *Machiavelli.* Past Master Series. New York: Hill and Wang, 1981. A concise and lucid introduction to Machiavelli's political philosophy that contains much fresh material.

Strauss, Leo. *Thoughts on Machiavelli.* Chicago: University of Chicago Press, 1958. A depiction of Machiavelli as a teacher of wickedness by one of the most renowned political scientists of our age.

Selected Bibliography

Tarlton, Charles D. *Fortune's Circle: A Biographical Interpretation of Niccolò Machiavelli.* A novel attempt to demonstrate how Machiavelli's writings may be used to shed light on his life.

Articles

Berlin, Isaiah. "The Originality of Machiavelli." In *Against the Current,* 25–79. London: Hogarth Press, 1979. A survey of more than a score of leading theories on how to interpret *The Prince* and the *Discourses.*

Clark, Richard C. "Machiavelli: Bibliographical Spectrum." *Review of National Literatures* 1 (1970): 93–135. An essential reference tool for any serious student of Machiavelli's thought.

Gilbert, Felix. "The Historian's Machiavelli." Part 2 in *History: Choice and Commitment,* 91–176. Cambridge, Mass.: Belknap Press of Harvard University Press, 1977. Four insightful essays on *The Prince,* the *Discourses, The Florentine History,* and Machiavellianism.

―――. "Machiavelli: The Renaissance of the Art of War." Chapter 1 in *Makers of Modern Strategy: Military Thought from Machiavelli to Hitler,* edited by Edward Mead Earle, 3–25. Princeton, N.J.: Princeton University Press, 1943. Reprint. Princeton, N.J.: Princeton University Press, 1971. A masterful assessment of Machiavelli's contribution to military science.

Gramsci, Antonio. "The Modern Prince." In *Selections from the Prison Notebooks of Antonio Gramsci,* edited and translated by Quintin Hoare and Geoffrey Nowell Smith, 123–205. London: Lawrence and Wishart, 1971. An analysis of the role of the Communist party as the "modern prince" by an internationally renowned Marxist thinker.

Hannaford, I. "Machiavelli's Concept of *Virtù* in *The Prince* and the *Discourses* Reconsidered." *Political Studies* 20 (1972): 185–89. An attempt to demonstrate that Machiavelli's concept of *virtù* is primarily civic rather than martial in character.

Strauss, Leo. "Machiavelli." In *History of Political Science,* 2d ed., edited by Leo Strauss and Joseph Cropsey, 271–92. Chicago: Rand-McNally, 1972. A final summation by one of Machiavelli's most sagacious critics.

Wood, Neal. "Machiavelli's Concept of *Virtù* Reconsidered." *Political Studies* 15 (1967): 159–72. Emphasizes the martial aspect of Machiavelli's concept of *virtù.*

Index

Agathocles of Syracuse, 59, 64–66
Alexander VI (pope), 4–5, 6–7, 35, 37, 42, 46–49, 56–57, 60, 62, 67–68
Amboise, Georges d' (cardinal of Rouen), 42
Apuleius, 105
Aristotle, 31, 32, 63

Bacon, Francis, 13
Boccaccio, Giovanni, 21, 27, 30
Borgia, Cesare, 5–7, 17, 37–39, 40, 42, 45–58, 62, 64, 74, 75, 87, 90, 97, 99, 115
Borja, Alonso de (cardinal and pope). *See* Calixtus III
Borja, Rodrigo Lanzol y (cardinal and pope). *See* Alexander VI
Bruni, Leonardo, 31, 32
Brutus, 33
Burnham, James, 16

Caesar, Julius, 29, 31, 33, 50, 83
Calixtus III (pope), 45–46, 49
Castiglione, Baldassare, 10, 52
Chance *(tychē)*, 63
Charles V of Germany (emperor of Holy Roman Empire), 9–10, 78–79
Charles VIII (king of France), 2–5, 34–37, 67, 72, 73, 77
Choice *(elezione)*, 90
Christie, Richard, 113–15
Cicero, 29, 61–62, 91–92
Clement VII (pope), 24–25, 78–81, 108
Corella, Michelotto da, 55, 75–76

Dante, 16, 21, 22, 27

Ease *(ozio)*, 105–6
Emerson, Ralph Waldo, 29
Erasmus, 9–10, 69

Ferdinand II of Aragon (king of Spain), 3, 39, 40, 49, 72
Fortune *(fortuna)*, 57, 59, 61, 62–64, 91, 93, 97, 106
Frederick the Great (king of Prussia), 111–12

Geis, Florence L., 113–14
Gentillet, Innocent, 109
Gramsci, Antonio, 15–16
Graves, Philip, 112
Guicciardini, Francesco, 12–13

Hannibal, 17, 86–90
Harrington, James, 13–14
Henry IV (king of France), 109–10

Imitation *(imitazione)*, 83
Index of Prohibited Books, 108–9

Jesuits. *See* Society of Jesus
Joly, Maurice, 112–13
Jonson, Ben, 110–11
Julius II (pope), 7, 23, 41, 57–58, 60, 68–70, 77

Leo X (pope), 22–24, 31, 68
Livy, 27–28, 30, 66, 71, 73, 87, 88, 102
Lorqua, Ramiro de, 50, 54–55
Louis XII (king of France), 5–7, 34–42, 49–51, 53, 56, 60–61, 74, 77

Macauley, Thomas Babington, 14–15
Machiavelli, Niccolò: *Art of War, The*, 24, 30, 71–72, 81, 83, 84; "Description of the Method Used by Duke Valentino in Killing Vitellozzo Vitelli, Oliverotto da Fermo, and Others," 56; "Discourse on Remodeling the Government of Florence," 31–32; *Discourses on the First Ten Books of Titus Livius*, 8, 26–33, 34, 66, 71, 73, 74, 82, 83, 89–91, 93–94, 96, 97, 100, 103–5; *Florentine History, The*, 24, 105, 106; *Golden Ass, The*, 105–7; *Life of Castruccio Castracani, The*, 64; *Mandrake, The*, 30; "Tercets on Ambition," 17, 99–100; "Tercets on Fortune," 63
Marlowe, Christopher, 110
Maugham, W. Somerset, 115
Maximilian I of Germany (emperor of Holy Roman Empire), 3, 6, 36, 61, 100
Medici, Catherine de (queen of France), 109
Medici, Giulio de' (cardinal and pope). *See* Clement VII
Medici, Giovanni de' (cardinal and pope). *See* Leo X
Medici, Lorenzo de' (duke of Urbino), 23–24, 29–30, 97
Medici, Lorenzo de' (the Magnificent), 1–2, 3, 22, 24, 109
Medici, Piero di Lorenzo de' (successor to Lorenzo the Magnificent), 3–4, 22–23, 36
Michelangelo, 23, 68, 80–81
Montaigne, Michel de, 17, 27
Moses, 59, 92–93
Mussolini, Benito, 10, 11

Nabis of Sparta, 66–67
Napoleon III (emperor of France), 112–13
Necessity *(necessità)*, 90, 100
Nietzsche, Friedrich, 17, 94–95
Numa (Roman king), 91, 92

O'Brien, Conor Cruise, 16–17, 99–100
Oliverotto da Fermo, 55, 56, 59, 64, 65, 67, 74

Petrarch, 21, 27, 98, 99

Index

Plutarch, 29
Pocock, John Greville Agard, 14
Polybius, 100–103, 107
Protocols of the Learned Elders of Zion, The, 112–13

Raab, Felix, 31
Raison d'état, 10, 109
Rienzi, Cola di, 98–99
Rousseau, Jean-Jacques, 15
Rovere, Giuliano della (cardinal and pope). *See* Julius II

Savonarola, Girolamo, 4–5, 6, 36
Scipio the Elder, 83, *87–90*
Scipio the Younger, 101

Sforza, Francesco, 59, 60
Sforza, Lodovico, 2–3, 39, 50, 60–61
Shakespeare, William, 110
Society of Jesus (Jesuits), 108
Soderini, Piero di Tommaso, 6, 7, 52, 75, 77, 78

Tiberius (Roman emperor), 62

Virtue *(virtù)*, 61, 62, 63–64, 65, 70, 83, 89, 90, 94, 105, 106
Vitelli, Vitellozzo, 52, 53, 55, 56, 65, 67, 74
Voltaire, 111–12

Webster, John, 115

The Author

Victor Anthony Rudowski holds the title of Professor Emeritus at Clemson University, where he has taught extensively in the humanities, as well as in world and comparative literature, while serving as a member of the Department of English. He earned an A.B. degree from Union College, Schenectady, New York, where he majored in philosophy, and a Ph.D. degree from Harvard University in Germanic languages and literatures. He is also the author of *Lessing's Aesthetica in Nuce: An Analysis of the May 26, 1769, Letter to Nicolai* (1971) and has published a number of articles on literary theory in such periodicals as *PMLA, Journal of the History of Ideas,* and the *Journal of Aesthetics and Art Criticism.*